DEVELOPMENTAL METHODOLOGY

Noel A. Card, University of Connecticut

WITH COMMENTARY BY

Paul E. Jose

Patricia J. Bauer
Series Editor

MONOGRAPHS OF THE SOCIETY FOR RESEARCH IN CHILD DEVELOPMENT

Serial No. 325, Vol. 82, No. 2, 2017

WILEY

Boston, Massachusetts   Oxford, United Kingdom

EDITOR
PATRICIA J. BAUER
Emory University

MANAGING EDITOR
LISA BRAVERMAN
Society for Research in Child Development

EDITORIAL ASSISTANT
STEPHANIE CUSTER
Society for Research in Child Development

DEVELOPMENTAL METHODOLOGY

CONTENTS

COMMENTARY

I. DEVELOPMENTAL METHODOLOGY AS A CENTRAL SUBDISCIPLINE OF DEVELOPMENTAL SCIENCE

Noel A. Card

This article is part of the issue "Developmental Methodology" Card (Issue Author). For a full listing of articles in this issue, see: http://onlinelibrary.wiley.com/doi/10.1111/mono.v82.2/issuetoc.

This first chapter introduces the main goals of the monograph and previews the remaining chapters. The goals of this monograph are to provide summaries of our current understanding of advanced developmental methodologies, provide information that can advance our understanding of human development, identify shortcomings in our understanding of developmental methodology, and serve as a flagpost for organizing developmental methodology as a subdiscipline within the broader field of developmental science. The remaining chapters in this monograph address issues in design (sampling and big data), longitudinal data analysis, and issues of replication and research accumulation. The final chapter describes the history of developmental methodology, considers how the previous chapters in this monograph fit within this subdiscipline, and offers recommendations for further advancement.

Scientific understanding of human development can advance only as far as the methodology used. For this reason, considerable attention has been devoted to research design, measurement, and data analysis among developmental scientists. Although this attention has often been loosely organized, there has recently been a trend of ordering this expertise within a subdiscipline of developmental science called "developmental methodology."

This monograph is an edited collection of chapters within the domain of developmental methodology that collectively share the following goals. First,

Corresponding author: Noel A. Card, University of Connecticut, Storrs, CT; email: noel.card@uconn.edu

DOI: 10.1111/mono.12295

this monograph provides updated and comprehensive, yet also accessible and brief, summaries of our current understanding of key methodologies used in developmental science. Second, this monograph describes how our current understanding can be further leveraged to advance understanding of human development. Third, this monograph identifies shortcomings in our understanding of developmental methodology in order to provide a roadmap for future methodological advances. Fourth, this monograph aims to serve as a flagpost for organizing developmental methodology as a subdiscipline within the broader field of developmental science. I elaborate further on each of these goals next.

Given the first goal of this monograph, to provide current summaries of key advanced developmental methodologies, each chapter is written by an expert in that particular area of developmental methodology. Despite the authors' expertise, the writing is intended for all developmental researchers, ranging from graduate students to seasoned scientists. Whenever feasible, technical information is referenced rather than described, and chapter authors aim for breadth more so than depth in their coverage (citing deeper treatments of specific topics).

Although this monograph is a collection of chapters by experts, and readers can turn to individual chapters depending on their interests, the collection of chapters represents a sum greater than the parts. Specifically, the chapters are arranged so that readers gain an appreciation of the breadth of developmental methodology. As will be elaborated below, the chapters cover foundational issues in design and measurement, latest advances in longitudinal analysis, and broader issues such as the places of big data and replication in developmental science. The integration of chapters into a coherent monograph is further facilitated by a common organization of chapters, cross-referencing of ideas, and consistency in balancing technical advances with accessibility. Thus, the collection of chapters in this monograph provides the reader with an updated and broad perspective on developmental methodology.

The second goal of this monograph is to provide practical information that can advance our understanding of human development. This goal builds upon previous, earlier efforts to do the same. In the late 1970s, Paul Baltes and John Nesselroade articulated many of the foundational issues of longitudinal data analysis and its role in developmental science. As described further in Chapter 4 of this volume, Baltes and Nesselroade (1979) identified five major goals of longitudinal analysis: to identify intraindividual (within-person) stability and change, to identify interindividual (between-person) differences in this intraindividual stability and change, to identify relationships of intraindividual change across constructs, to identify the determinants of intraindividual change, and to identify the determinants of interindividual differences in intraindividual change. This articulation of goals of longitudinal analysis greatly impacted developmental science, to the point that nearly half (41% in a survey by Card & Little, 2007) of articles published in leading developmental journals use longitudinal data.

The progression of analysis techniques for longitudinal data has continued since this time, with many influential books (e.g., Collins & Horn, 1991; Little, Bovaird, & Card, 2007; Singer & Willett, 2003) offering developmental researchers accessible introductions to advanced analytic techniques (for a lengthier description of this history of progress, see Chapter 8 of this volume). Importantly, attention was also broadened beyond analysis issues to better consider theory, design, and measurement (e.g., Collins, 2006; McCartney, Burchinal, & Bub, 2006), thus offering researchers a more complete set of tools for improving the methodological rigor of developmental science. The current monograph seeks to continue this traditional by explicating how the methodological tools described in each chapter can directly improve our studies of developmental processes. When available, examples of these applications to the study of human development are mentioned. In short, these chapters avoid disciplinary agnosticism; that is, technical descriptions that are not tailored to developmental science. Instead, each chapter presents a perspective rooted in both methodology and developmental science.

The third goal of this monograph is to identify shortcomings in our understanding of developmental methodology. Like other areas in developmental science, developmental methodology is continuously evolving, overturning earlier practices, and resolving differences of opinion. This third goal represents an important advancement denoting the maturity of developmental methodology: it is no longer the case that developmental researchers are simply learning the techniques developed by methodologists, but developmental science is prompting new challenges and advancement of methodologies. In other words, the flow of information is no longer methodology→developmental science, but rather methodology→developmental science. Chapter authors describe this fluid state of their topics, and make recommendations for the most important methodological advances to come.

The fourth goal of this monograph is to serve as a flagpost for organizing developmental methodology as a subdiscipline within the broader field of developmental science. The metaphor of a "flagpost" denotes four ideas. First, the choice of topics for this monograph ranging from issues of design, analysis, and progression of developmental science, mark out some of what I believe are the most active and important contemporary topics in developmental methodology. Others may have different perspectives on the most important topics, and I acknowledge that these may be just as important as those selected for this monograph. Perhaps expanding the metaphor to plural—multiple "flag posts"—is therefore appropriate. Second, flags can serve the purpose of drawing attention in a direction and, whether the metaphor is of a single or multiple flagposts, I hope that this monograph draws attention to the importance, value, and challenges of using advanced methodologies to improve the rigor of developmental science. Third, a flagpost can serve as a gathering point. Here, the metaphor might denote another function of this monograph, of making salient the growing number of developmental scientists using and advancing methodologies. By increasing the salience of these individuals, I hope to solidify developmental methodology as an active and important subdiscipline of developmental science. Finally, at risk of taking a single metaphor too far, I point out that a flagpost can signal a general location without clear boundaries, which I think is appropriate for developmental methodology. This subdiscipline should not be an exclusive group; instead, all scholars and researchers wishing to use rigorous methodologies to advance understanding of human development might be considered developmental methodologists.

Our (the editor's and all chapter authors') hope is that this monograph, alongside other recent works (e.g., developmental methodology conferences organized by Card and Little; a *Handbook of Developmental Research Methods* edited by Laursen, Little, & Card, 2012), will facilitate discussion about the unique opportunities and challenges of scientists committed to developing and using advanced methods within developmental science. It builds upon an earlier monograph (e.g., McCartney et al., 2006) to provide an update within a rapidly changing subdiscipline, yet is accessible enough to be of benefit to most readers. Thus, this monograph serves as an invitation to all developmental scientists to come a few steps toward the flagpost of developmental methodology.

CONTENT OF THE MONOGRAPH

The chapters of this monograph were selected to identify major themes of developmental methodology, broadly defined to encompass issues of design, analysis, and research progression. Besides covering a wide range of topics, chapters were selected that (i) represent active areas of research or debate, (ii) are important in advancing the quality of developmental science, and (iii) seem likely to remain active and important areas of developmental methodology in the foreseeable future. Following this first introductory chapter, the monograph consists of seven chapters. The first two chapters focus primarily on design issues. In Chapter 2, Jager, Putnick, and Bornstein consider the merits of different sampling strategies. In Chapter 3, Davis-Kean and Jager describe the use of large-scale data sets in developmental science. Both of these chapters connect with the second and fifth rationales of longitudinal research described in Chapter 4 (while Chapter 3 also considers the second rationale), and these chapters also represent both persistent

(Chapter 2) and more recent (Chapter 3) design decisions that all developmental scientists must consider.

In Chapters 4, 5, and 6, attention shifts to issues in longitudinal design and analysis issues that are central to developmental science. Grimm, Davoudzadeh, and Ram (Chapter 4) begin this section by providing an overview of longitudinal analyses in developmental science, which clearly articulates the five rationales for conducting longitudinal analysis and the value of each for developmental science. Rush and Hofer (Chapter 5) then describe considerations in measurement within longitudinal studies; although the topic of measurement is long-standing in developmental science, the authors attention to measurement within intensive longitudinal designs emphasizes the importance of studying intraindividual stability and change (the first, third, and fourth rationales described in Chapter 4). Finally, Rovine and Lo (Chapter 6) describe person-specific longitudinal approaches, again emphasizing attention to intraindividual stability and change (the first, second, and fourth rationales). This attention to intraindividual stability and change represents a shift from the heavy emphasis on interindividual differences that has dominated much of developmental science, resulting in a more equitable balance of attention on both intraindividual and interindividual stability, change, and determinants of change.

In Chapter 7, Card considers the broader issues of replication and research accumulation in developmental science. This focus goes beyond the individual study to consider broader issues in developmental science. The final chapter, by Little, Wang, and Gorrall (Chapter 8), describes the history of developmental methodology, considers how the previous chapters in this monograph fit within this subdiscipline, and offers recommendations for further advancement.

Collectively, these chapters cover many important and active areas in developmental methodology. Our hope is that you will find them informative and that they will generate further activity in developmental methodology and the broader discipline of developmental science.

REFERENCES

Baltes, P. B., & Nesselroade, J. R. (1979). History and rationale of longitudinal research. In J. R. Nesselroade & P. B. Baltes (Eds.), *Longitudinal research in the study of behavior and development* (pp. 1–39). New York, NY: Academic Press.

Card, N. A., & Little, T. D. (2007). Longitudinal modeling of developmental processes. *International Journal of Behavioral Development*, **31**, 297–302.

Collins, L. M. (2006). Analysis of longitudinal data: The integration of theoretical models, temporal design, and statistical model. *Annual Review of Psychology*, **57**, 505–528.

Collins, L. M., & Horn, J. L. (1991). *Best methods for the analysis of change: Recent advances, unanswered questions, future directions.* Washington, DC: American Psychological Association.

Laursen, B., Little, T. D., & Card, N. A. (2012). *Handbook of developmental research methods.* New York, NY: Guilford Press.

Little, T. D., Bovaird, J. A., & Card, N. A. (2007). *Modeling ecological and contextual effects in longitudinal studies.* Mahwah, NJ: Erlbaum Press.

McCartney, K., Burchinal, M. R., & Bub, K. L. (2006). Best practices in quantitative methods for developmentalists. *Monographs of the Society for Research in Child Development, 71* (3).

Singer, J. D., & Willett, J. B. (2003). *Applied longitudinal data analysis: Modeling change and event occurrence.* New York, NY: Oxford University Press.

II. MORE THAN JUST CONVENIENT: THE SCIENTIFIC MERITS OF HOMOGENEOUS CONVENIENCE SAMPLES

Justin Jager, Diane L. Putnick, and Marc H. Bornstein

This article is part of the issue "Developmental Methodology" Card (Issue Author). For a full listing of articles in this issue, see: http://onlinelibrary.wiley.com/doi/10.1111/mono.v82.2/issuetoc.

Despite their disadvantaged generalizability relative to probability samples, nonprobability convenience samples are the standard within developmental science, and likely will remain so because probability samples are cost-prohibitive and most available probability samples are ill-suited to examine developmental questions. In lieu of focusing on how to eliminate or sharply reduce reliance on convenience samples within developmental science, here we propose how to augment their advantages when it comes to understanding population effects as well as subpopulation differences. Although all convenience samples have less clear generalizability than probability samples, we argue that homogeneous convenience samples have clearer generalizability relative to conventional convenience samples. Therefore, when researchers are limited to convenience samples, they should consider homogeneous convenience samples as a positive alternative to conventional (or heterogeneous) convenience samples. We discuss future directions as well as potential obstacles to expanding the use of homogeneous convenience samples in developmental science.

The roots of sociodemographic differences—including sexual orientation, gender, ethnicity, urbanicity, SES, culture, and nationality—in

Corresponding author: Justin Jager, T. Denny Sanford School of Social and Family Dynamics, Arizona State University, PO Box 873701, Tempe, AZ 85287-3701; email: justin.jager@asu.edu

This research was supported by the Intramural Research Program of the NIH, NICHD.

DOI: 10.1111/mono.12296

13

developmental processes and trends are complex and likely the product of layered interactions among biological, behavioral, and sociocultural factors (Bettencourt & Lopez, 1993; Crimmins & Saito, 2001; Jager, 2011; Jager & Davis-Kean, 2011; Phinney, 1996). Nonetheless, they are important to unpack because without a scientific base of knowledge regarding human health and behavior that takes into account the sociodemographic diversity of the population, health care delivery, planning, and policymaking would be compromised by inadequate information and potentially misleading generalizations (Bettencourt & Lopez, 1993; Mays, Ponce, Washington, & Cochran, 2003).

For this reason, a sizable amount of developmental science research is devoted to understanding developmental processes and trends in specific sociodemographic groups as well as differences across two or more sociodemographic groups. Despite their disadvantages in generalizability relative to probability samples, much of this research relies on convenience samples—a fact that does not bode well for the field of developmental science (Bornstein, Jager, & Putnick, 2013). Developmental scientists should rely more on probability samples, for reasons we describe below. Nonetheless, because convenience samples are commonly used, we focus here on how developmental scientists can limit the disadvantages of convenience samples when it comes to understanding population effects as well as subpopulation differences. As we outline below, relative to conventional (or heterogeneous) convenience samples (i.e., samples that are open to all sociodemographic subgroups), homogeneous convenience samples (i.e., samples that are intentionally limited to specific sociodemographic subgroups and, therefore, homogeneous on one or more sociodemographic factors) should, on average, yield estimates with clearer, albeit narrower, generalizability and, therefore, provide more accurate accounts of population effects and subpopulation differences. On this basis, we argue that when researchers are limited to convenience samples, they should adopt homogeneous convenience samples as a positive alternative to conventional convenience samples.

Before distinguishing between conventional and homogeneous convenience samples, we compare and contrast convenience sampling in general with probability sampling and then, using an illustration, discuss in more depth the key disadvantage of all convenience samples: due to poor generalizability they often yield biased estimates of the target population and its sociodemographic subpopulations. Next, we describe conventional and homogeneous convenience sampling, and explain why, of the two, homogeneous convenience sampling provides clearer generalizability and, therefore, a more accurate account of its target population effects and subpopulation differences. We conclude by discussing future directions as well as potential obstacles to expanding the use of homogeneous convenience samples within developmental science.

PROBABILITY SAMPLING VERSUS CONVENIENCE SAMPLING

Within developmental science, sampling strategies generally fall into two broad categories: nonprobability sampling and probability sampling (Bornstein et al., 2013; Levy & Lemeshow, 2011). Probability sampling strategies are any methods of sampling that utilize some form of random selection, which entails setting up a process or procedure that assures that different members of the target population have equal probabilities of being chosen. Probability sampling strategies include simple random sampling as well as more complex sampling designs such as stratified sampling and cluster sampling (and its variants such as probability proportional to size sampling; see Bornstein et al., 2013; Cochran, 1977; Levy & Lemeshow, 2011). The key advantage of probability sampling strategies is that they all, when carried out properly, should yield an unbiased sample that is representative of the target population. As a result, researchers can safely assume that estimates obtained from probability samples are both unbiased and generalizable. The key disadvantage of probability sampling strategies is that they present a significant challenge to execute. That is, the sizes of probability samples need to be quite large, often coming at great costs in terms of money, time, and effort. Moreover, designing probability samples requires substantial expertise. Indeed, due to the costs and challenges associated with probability samples, many of the prominent probability samples within developmental science are managed by federal agencies or large research centers with substantial annual budgets, such as Add Health (http://www.cpc.unc.edu/projects/addhealth) and the Early Childhood Longitudinal Program (ECLS; http://nces.ed.gov/ecls). Furthermore, as Davis-Kean and Jager (Chapter 3, this volume) discuss in more detail, most existing probability samples are ill-suited to examine developmental questions.

Nonprobability sampling strategies are any methods of sampling that do not utilize some form of random selection. By far the most common nonprobability sampling strategy used within developmental science is convenience sampling (for review see Bornstein et al., 2013), which is a sampling strategy where participants are selected in an ad hoc fashion based on their accessibility and/or proximity to the research. One of the most common examples of convenience sampling within developmental science is the use of student volunteers as study participants. The key advantages of convenience sampling are that it is cheap, efficient, and simple to implement. The key disadvantage of convenience sampling is that the sample lacks clear generalizability. Moreover, these advantages and disadvantages apply, albeit in varying degrees, to all types of convenience samples. Therefore, the advantages and disadvantages of convenience sampling are the reverse of probability sampling. Whereas probability samples yield results with clearer generalizability, convenience samples are far less expensive, more efficient, and simpler to execute.

Even though probability sampling is more advantaged in terms of scientific merit (i.e., probability sampling yields samples with clearer generalizability), convenience samples are the norm within developmental science. Bornstein et al. (2013) tallied the use of probability sampling and different types of nonprobability sampling from 2007 to 2011 in five prominent developmental science journals. Among the studies for which the type of sampling strategy could be conclusively determined, 92.5% utilized a convenience sample. Probability sampling accounted for only 5.5% of studies. Thus, from a tally of recent publications in prestigious journals in developmental science, convenience samples were the norm and were over 16 times more likely to be used than probability samples.

POOR GENERALIZABILITY LEADS TO ESTIMATE BIAS: AN ILLUSTRATION

Because the generalizability of convenience samples is unclear, the estimates derived from convenience samples are often biased (i.e., sample estimates are not reflective of true effects among the target population because the sample poorly represents the target population). This bias extends to estimates of population effects as well as estimates of subpopulation differences. We illustrate these effects by outlining the known population parameters for the association between harsh parenting and externalizing as well as ethnic differences in that association, and then compare known population parameters to estimates obtained from three hypothetical convenience samples.

For the purposes of this illustration, we use the following target population: White and Black youth between the ages of 10 and 19 in the United States. Based on data from the United States Census and research on the association between harsh parenting and externalizing in this target population, we know the population parameters of the association between harsh parenting and externalizing with some confidence; they are listed in the first row of Table 1. Specifically, based on the 2010 United States Census (2012), the White–Black breakdown is roughly 80%/20%. Based on studies utilizing national probability samples of children and adolescents, the effect size (Cohen's d) for the White–Black difference in the income-to-needs ratio, a common indicator of socioeconomic status (SES), is around 1.0 (Davis-Kean & Sexton, 2009; Geronimus, Bound, Keene, & Hicken, 2007). For ease of interpretation, SES is centered around the population mean and has an SD of 1.0. Consequently, given the White–Black population breakdown of 80%/ 20% and the effect size of 1.0 for the White–Black difference in income-to-needs ratio, mean SES for the White population = 0.2 and mean SES for the Black population = −.8 (i.e., the difference between the White and Black means equals 1.0 and the weighted average of the White and Black means is 0). Based on extant research, among the total population (i.e., White and

TABLE 1

Population Parameters and Sample Estimates for the Association Between Harsh Parenting and Externalizing Among White and Black Adolescents

| | Demographic Characteristics | | | | | | Association Between Harsh Parenting and Externalizing | | | | | | | |
| | Representation | | Socioeconomic Status | | | Ethnicity | Population Parameters (ρ) | | | | Sample Estimates (r) | | | |
	White (%)	Black (%)	Total	White	Black	d	ρ	ρ^w	ρ^b	$\rho^w - \rho^b$	r	r^w	r^b	$r^w - r^b$
Target population	80	20	0.00	0.20	−0.80	1.0	0.25	0.30	0.10	0.20				
Sample A: high White, high SES	95	5	1.20	1.23	0.63	0.6					0.39	0.40	0.15	0.25
Sample B: high Black, low SES	30	70	−1.20	−0.99	−1.29	0.3					0.11	0.18	0.08	0.10
Sample C: high SES White, low SES Black	80	20	0.90	1.50	−1.50	3.0					0.36	0.43	0.07	0.36

Note. Assuming $N = 500$, w = White; b = Black, Ethnicity d = White-Black difference in socioeconomic status.

17

Black combined) harsh parenting is positively correlated with externalizing ($\rho \approx 0.25$; Bailey, Hill, Oesterle, & Hawkins, 2009; Burnette, Oshri, Lax, Richards, & Ragbeer, 2012; Rothbaum & Weisz, 1994). Finally, although some research suggests no ethnic difference in association between harsh parenting and externalizing (Berlin et al., 2009; Gershoff, Lansford, Sexton, Davis-Kean, & Sameroff, 2012; McLoyd & Smith, 2002), we focus on the substantial amount of research that suggests the association is higher for White children ($\rho^w \approx 0.30$) than for Black children ($\rho^b \approx 0.10$; Deater-Deckard, Dodge, Bates, & Pettit, 1996; Gunnoe & Mariner, 1997; Lansford, Deater-Deckard, Dodge, Bates, & Pettit, 2004). For the purposes of illustration, imagine that for both ethnic groups the association between harsh parenting and externalizing increases as levels of SES increase, but does so more for White adolescents ($\rho^w = 0.280 + 0.100^*SES$)[1] than for Black adolescents ($\rho^b = 0.128 + 0.035$ $^*SES$)[2]. Although hypothetical, such an interaction is plausible because ethnicity and SES often interact with one another to inform psychosocial outcomes (Desimone, 1999; Kessler & Neighbors, 1986). The association between harsh parenting and externalizing across levels of SES ($\pm 2.0\ SD$) is graphed for each ethnic group in Figure 1; as the level of SES increases, the ethnic difference in the association between harsh parenting and externalizing also increases.

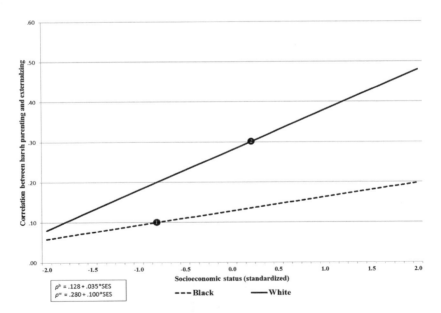

Figure 1.—Correlation between harsh parenting and externalizing, by ethnicity and SES. ● = population parameter (i.e., $\rho^b = 0.10$) for the Black adolescent population, for which mean SES = $-.8$ (i.e., $0.10 = 0.128 + .035^* - .8$). ◕ = population parameter (i.e., $\rho^w = 0.30$) for the White adolescent population, for which mean SES = 0.2 (i.e., $0.30 = 0.280 + 0.100^*0.2$).

To devise hypothetical convenience samples, we use school-based samples as a heuristic. We do so because in developmental science a common sampling frame (e.g., the set of participants from which a sample is drawn) for convenience samples is a particular school or a particular school district, and schools and school districts can vary dramatically from one another in terms of ethnic and socioeconomic distribution. The demographic characteristics and sample estimates for each of three hypothetical convenience samples are listed in Table 1. In Sample A ("High White, High SES"), both White adolescents and those of higher SES are overrepresented, and the ethnic difference in SES is 40% smaller relative to the target population. In Sample B ("High Black, Low SES"), Black adolescents and those of lower SES are overrepresented, and the ethnic difference in SES is 70% smaller relative to the target population. Finally, in Sample C (High SES White, Low SES Black), each of the two ethnic groups is properly represented; however, among White adolescents those of higher SES are overrepresented, whereas among Black adolescents those of lower SES are overrepresented. As a result, in Sample C, the ethnic difference in SES is three times larger than it is in the target population.

When considered individually, all three convenience samples yield misleading or biased estimates of the overall population effect (i.e., $r \neq \rho$) and of the subpopulation difference (i.e., $[r^w - r^b] \neq [\rho^w - \rho^b]$). Specifically, because White adolescents and adolescents of higher SES are overrepresented in Sample A and ρ is higher among White adolescents and those of higher SES, ρ is overestimated in Sample A ($r = 0.39$). Also, because $[\rho^w - \rho^b]$ is larger among adolescents of higher SES (Figure 1), and adolescents of higher SES are overrepresented in Sample A, $[r^w - r^b]$ is also overestimated in Sample A ($[r^w - r^b] = 0.25$). The estimates for Sample B are also biased; whereas the estimates for Sample A are too high, the estimates for Sample B are too low. Because Black adolescents and adolescents of lower SES are overrepresented in Sample B and ρ is lower among Black adolescents and adolescents of lower SES, ρ is underestimated in Sample B ($r = 0.11$). Also, because $[\rho^w - \rho^b]$ is smaller among those of lower SES (Figure 1), and those of lower SES are overrepresented in Sample B, $[\rho^w - \rho^b]$ is also underestimated in Sample B ($[r^w - r^b] = 0.10$). Finally, because ρ is particularly high among high-SES White adolescents, and high-SES adolescents are overrepresented in the White subsample of Sample C, both ρ and ρ^w are overestimated in Sample C ($r = 0.36$; $r^w = 0.43$). Whereas ρ^w is overestimated in Sample C, ρ^b ($r^b = .07$) is underestimated in Sample C (because high-SES adolescents are underrepresented among the Black subsample), and as a result $[\rho^w - \rho^b]$ is overestimated in Sample C ($[r^w - r^b] = 0.36$).

When considered collectively, how would researchers integrate the findings from these three convenience samples? Their estimates of population effects and subpopulation differences are inconsistent; therefore, they cannot all be correct estimates of the same target population. But is one sample's set of estimates more valid (or less invalid) than the others? Because we know the true population parameters for our example, here we are able to judge the validity of each sample's estimates. But for most scientific investigations using convenience samples to study a given developmental process, the true population parameters of the target population are not known (If the true population parameters were known, then there would be no reason to undertake the study in the first place). Therefore, when attempting to integrate inconsistent findings across a set of studies using convenience samples, investigations typically do not have the known population parameters to use as a benchmark. Although this example involved a set of hypothetical studies, substantial variation in the sociodemographic composition of convenience samples is all too common across studies examining a given developmental characteristic in an equivalent target population. Importantly, these variations make it difficult to determine whether inconsistencies across studies represent true population differences or instead are artifacts of differences in sample composition. Put succinctly, science is supposed to be cumulative; however, the use of convenience samples can translate into across-study inconsistencies that are difficult to integrate and, therefore, build upon.

CONVENTIONAL VERSUS HOMOGENEOUS CONVENIENCE SAMPLING

Despite their disadvantaged generalizability, convenience samples are the standard within developmental science, and likely will remain so because probability samples are cost-prohibitive and most probability samples are ill-suited to examine developmental questions. Instead of focusing on how to reduce the use of convenience samples within developmental science, we focus here on how to limit their disadvantages when it comes to understanding population effects as well as subpopulation differences. Although all convenience samples have less clear generalizability than probability samples, not all convenience samples are the same, and some convenience samples have clearer generalizability than others. We argue that homogeneous convenience samples have clearer generalizability relative to conventional convenience samples. In developmental science, homogeneous convenience samples are far less common than conventional convenience samples. Therefore, we believe that one way to minimize the disadvantages of convenience samples is through the strategic use of homogeneous convenience samples in place of conventional convenience samples. Below, we describe in more detail what we mean by conventional and homogeneous convenience samples, and then we describe why, of the two, homogeneous convenience sampling has clearer generalizability. Next, we describe their advantages and disadvantages when it comes to estimating population effects as well as subpopulation differences.

Conventional Convenience Samples

The sampling frame for conventional convenience samples is not intentionally constrained based on sociodemographic background (i.e., participants of all sociodemographic backgrounds are eligible for participation). For example, aside from the fact that they were limited to two ethnic groups for the sake of simplicity, the three hypothetical convenience samples listed in Table 1 are conventional convenience samples. For these samples, the sampling frame was truly ad hoc (regardless of sociodemographics, all were welcome to participate provided they volunteered). We refer to these types of convenience samples as "conventional" because they are by far the most common type of convenience sample in developmental science; however, these types of convenience samples can also be conceptualized as *heterogeneous* convenience samples because, by design, the expectation is heterogeneity (i.e., diversity) in all sociodemographic factors. As part of their tally of the types of sampling strategies within developmental science, Bornstein et al. (2013) found that among the studies that utilized a convenience sample, 89% were conventional convenience samples.

Homogeneous Convenience Samples

In contrast to conventional convenience sampling, the sampling frame for homogeneous convenience sampling is intentionally constrained with respect to sociodemographic background. In homogeneous convenience sampling, researchers undertake to study (and therefore sample) a population that is homogeneous with respect to one or more sociodemographic factors (e.g., the overall population is composed of just Blacks or Whites). Thus, the target population (not just the sample studied) is a specific sociodemographic subgroup. For example, for a sample that is homogeneous with respect to ethnic group, the sampling frame is limited to, say, just Black Americans, and only Black Americans are sampled. Homogeneous samples can differ in their degree of sociodemographic homogeneity. For example, the target population and its matching sample could be limited to one sociodemographic factor such as ethnicity (e.g., Black Americans); two sociodemographic factors such as SES and ethnicity (e.g., affluent Black Americans); three sociodemographic factors, such as gender, SES, and ethnicity (e.g., female, affluent, Black Americans), and so forth. The greater the number of homogeneous sociodemographic factors, the more homogeneous the sample and the narrower the sampling frame. Although relatively rare, homogeneous samples are used in developmental science, often to examine underrepresented sociodemographic groups (e.g., ethnic or sexual minorities). As part of their tally of the types of sampling strategies in developmental science, Bornstein et al. (2013) found that among the studies that utilized a convenience sample, only 8.6% were homogeneous convenience samples.

The key advantage of homogeneous convenience samples, relative to conventional convenience samples, is their clearer generalizability. Because the sampling frame of homogeneous convenience samples is more homogeneous than the sampling frame for conventional convenience samples, researchers can be more confident with respect to generalizability. Why does a more homogeneous sampling frame translate into clearer generalizability? Logic dictates that the more homogeneous a population, the easier (more probable) it is to generate a representative sample, even when using convenience sampling. Therefore, by intentionally constraining the sampling frame to reduce the amount of sociodemographic heterogeneity, the chance of bias in sampling, as it relates to sociodemographic characteristics of the target population, is reduced (although not all together eliminated).

Imagine two different convenience samples that seek to examine the same developmental process. Each convenience sample consists of 500 families, and both samples are taken from the same large Midwestern city. The first is a conventional convenience sample and, because it does not limit its sampling frame with respect to any sociodemographic factors, contains at least some amount of heterogeneity on many sociodemographic factors. The second is a homogeneous convenience sample and, because it limits its sampling frame with respect to ethnicity (only samples Black families), SES (only samples middle-class families), and national origin (only samples families within which both birth parents were born in the United States), it contains no heterogeneity on these sociodemographic factors. Now, imagine that the findings differed between the two samples, which would not be surprising given the stark sociodemographic differences between the two samples. Which sample's findings would have clearer generalizability? In our view, the findings from the homogeneous convenience sample would have the clearer generalizability. That is, we could be more confident that the findings from the homogeneous convenience sample generalize to middle-class, native-born, Black families than we could be that the findings from the conventional convenience sample generalize to all families (regardless of ethnicity, class, or national origin). This confidence is because, in comparison to the conventional convenience sample, the homogeneous convenience sample should, on average, have a sociodemographic distribution that more closely reflects the sociodemographic distribution of its target population, and therefore, its estimates of its target population should, on average, be more accurate, precise, and valid.

The key disadvantage of homogeneous convenience samples, relative to conventional convenience samples, is their narrower generalizability. Although homogeneous convenience samples have clearer generalizability, their findings also generalize to a more circumscribed population. Returning to the example above, although the findings from the homogeneous convenience sample of middle-class, native-born, Black families have clearer generalizability than do the findings from the conventional convenience sample of all families, the findings from the homogeneous convenience sample, at best, only generalize to middle-class, native-born, Black families. Therefore, the findings from the homogeneous convenience sample reveal very little if anything about families that are not middle-class, native-born, and Black. Another disadvantage of homogeneous convenience samples is that, if they are samples of underrepresented sociodemographic groups, they can be more costly and time consuming relative to conventional convenience samples. For example, more effort is involved in recruiting 350 Gay/Lesbian adolescents of Hispanic descent from lower class families than is involved in recruiting 350 adolescents of any sexual orientation, ethnicity, or social class. Finally, as is the case for all types of sampling, clearly and accurately defining one's target population is essential for homogeneous convenience sampling to be effective. After all, to maximize the alignment (and therefore generalizability) between a sample and its target population, researchers must have a firm and detailed understanding of their target population.

Although the generalizability of homogeneous convenience samples is clearer, if narrower, relative to conventional convenience samples, we emphasize that both homogeneous convenience samples and conventional convenience samples have poor generalizability relative to probability samples. On a hypothetical continuum of generalizability, probability samples are at one end and conventional convenience samples are at the other end. Homogeneous convenience samples fall somewhere in between, although likely closer to conventional convenience samples. However, the more homogeneous they are (i.e., the more sociodemographic factors that are homogeneous), the closer they fall in terms of generalizability to probability samples. Again though, the more homogeneous they are, the narrower their generalizability. Therefore, with respect to the estimation of population effects, homogeneous convenience samples should, on average, provide more accurate population estimates, albeit of a more circumscribed population. We now turn to the implications of these arguments for the estimation of subpopulation differences.

Homogeneous Samples and Subpopulation Differences

If a homogeneous convenience sample is homogeneous with respect to the sociodemographic factor of interest, then homogeneous convenience samples are ill-suited for directly examining sociodemographic differences (e.g., a convenience sample homogeneous with respect to ethnicity is not equipped to examine ethnic differences). However, relative to conventional convenience samples, homogeneous convenience samples are better-suited

TABLE 2

SOCIODEMOGRAPHIC CHARACTERISTICS OF HYPOTHETICAL CONVENIENCE SAMPLES, BY SES, ETHNICITY, AND TYPE OF CONVENIENCE SAMPLE

Ethnicity	SES		
	Low	Medium	High
(a) Conventional convenience samples			
Ethnicity			
Black	30% White/70% Black M SES = −1.5 SES range = −2.5 to 2.5	25% White/75% Black M SES = 0.0 SES range = −2.5 to 2.5	15% White/85% Black M SES = 1.5 SES range = −2.5 to 2.5
White	90% White/10% Black M SES = −1.5 SES range = −2.5 to 2.5	92% White/8% Black M SES = 0.0 SES range = −2.5 to 2.5	88% White/12% Black M SES = 1.5 SES range = −2.5 to 2.5
(b) Homogeneous convenience samples			
Ethnicity			
Black	0% White/100% Black M SES = −1.5 SES range = −2.5 to −1.0	0% White/100% Black M SES = 0.0 SES range = >−1.0 to <1.0	0% White/100% Black M SES = 1.5 SES range = 1.0 to 2.5
White	100% White/0% Black M SES = −1.5 SES range = −2.5 to −1.0	100% White/0% Black M SES = 0.0 SES range = >−1.0 to <1.0	100% White/0% Black M SES = 1.5 SES range = 1.0 to 2.5

Note. For each conventional convenience sample, participants from all levels of Ethnicity and SES are represented to some extent. For example, among the Low SES/Black conventional convenience sample, although the sample is disproportionately Black, both ethnic groups are included and, although the average SES is −1.5, there are some participants with Medium (>−1.0 to <1.0) and High SES (1.0 to 2.5) as well. For each homogeneous convenience sample, participants from only a single level of ethnicity and SES are represented. For example, among the Low SES/Black homogeneous convenience sample, the sample is limited to only Black respondents and only those with Low SES (−2.5 to −1.0).

24

to address sociodemographic differences when aggregating across a series of studies. Consider the six conventional convenience samples listed in Table 2a. Like the three convenience samples in Table 1, each of the six samples in Table 2a is heterogeneous with respect to both ethnicity and SES and all six samples have varying sociodemographic representation with respect to ethnicity and SES. As was the case for the three convenience samples in Table 1, likely the six conventional convenience samples in Table 2a would yield conflicting findings. These conflicting findings would be difficult to explain because there is ethnic and SES heterogeneity both within and across the samples. The reasoning is similar to that of a 2*3 ANOVA, with ethnicity (Black and White) and SES (low, middle, high) as the two factors. In this example, the ANOVA would have six cells just as Table 2a has six cells. Within an ANOVA, for the between-factor variance to be separated from the within-factor variance each cell must be homogeneous with respect to both factors (i.e., all variance in factors is across-cell). The problem with conventional convenience samples is that there is heterogeneity for both sociodemographic factors (i.e., ethnicity and SES) within each of the six samples as well as heterogeneity for both factors across the six samples. As a result, it is difficult to parse exactly how, if at all, ethnicity and SES heterogeneity contribute to between-sample differences in findings.

Next, consider the six homogeneous convenience samples listed in Table 2b. Each of the six homogeneous convenience samples is homogeneous with respect to both ethnicity and SES; however, they vary as to which ethnic group and which category of SES is homogeneous. Like the six conventional convenience samples, the six homogeneous convenience samples would likely yield conflicting findings, but unlike the six conventional convenience samples, for the six homogeneous convenience samples any between-sample differences in findings could be reasonably attributed to ethnic and/or SES heterogeneity. Because all ethnic and SES heterogeneity is between-sample for the homogeneous convenience samples, between-sample differences in findings can be more clearly attributed to ethnic and SES heterogeneity, or at least they can be with greater confidence relative to the conventional convenience samples. Thus, when considered individually each of the six homogeneous convenience samples has narrower but clearer generalizability than each of the six conventional convenience samples, and when considered collectively the homogeneous convenience samples also provide a more accurate and encompassing account of sociodemographic differences than do conventional convenience samples.

If a homogeneous convenience sample is heterogeneous with respect to the sociodemographic factor of interest, then it is well-suited for directly examining sociodemographic differences. For example, a homogeneous convenience sample that is homogeneous with respect to SES, but heterogeneous with respect to ethnicity, is well-suited to examine ethnic differences because more than one ethnic group can be compared, while holding SES constant. Moreover, the key advantage (i.e., clearer generalizability) and disadvantage (narrower generalizability) of homogeneous convenience samples relative to conventional convenience samples would also apply to the examination of sociodemographic differences. However, like conventional convenience samples, homogeneous convenience samples may lack sufficient power to detect group differences, leading to Type II errors. Imagine a homogeneous convenience sample ($N = 200$) that matches the first data column in Table 2b such that it is heterogeneous in ethnicity (includes White and Black adolescents) and homogeneous with respect to SES (includes only low-SES adolescents or those with SES < -1.0). Because Black adolescents represent only 20% of the population, only 40 Black participants would be expected in the sample. For example, based on $\alpha = 0.05$, in an ANOVA design with two groups (or an independent samples t test) this homogeneous convenience sample yields sufficient power (≥ 0.80) to detect Black–White differences provided the effect size (d) is ≥ 0.50 (where power is determined by $\delta = d*\sqrt{(n_1 n_2)/(n_1 + n_2)}$; Faul, Erdfelder, Lang, & Buchner, 2007).

An alternative to a homogeneous convenience sample would be a quota homogeneous convenience sample. In quota sampling, another form of nonprobability sampling, fixed numbers of participants from different sociodemographic groups are recruited, typically using convenience sampling (e.g., separate samples of White and Black adolescents, each of which are convenience samples of 100 individuals). Returning to the example above, imagine a homogeneous convenience sample ($N = 200$) that matches the first data column in Table 2b such that it is heterogeneous with respect to ethnicity (includes both White and Black adolescents), homogeneous with respect to SES (includes only low-SES adolescents or those with SES < -1.0), but includes equal numbers of White and Black adolescents. Based on $\alpha = .05$, in an ANOVA design with two groups this quota homogeneous convenience sample yields sufficient power (≥ 0.80) to detect Black–White differences provided the effect size (d) is ≥ 0.40, which translates into a 20% reduction in the size of the minimally detectable effect relative to the homogeneous convenience sample.

LOOKING FORWARD

Despite their disadvantaged generalizability relative to probability samples, convenience samples are the standard within developmental science, and likely will remain so because probability samples are cost-prohibitive and most available probability samples are ill-suited to examine developmental questions. The advantaged generalizability of probability samples is both important and well-documented within the sampling literature, but it obscures the fact that, in terms of generalizability, some convenience samples are less disadvantaged than others. Therefore, in addition to comparing and contrasting the merits of probability samples with convenience samples, we believe that the field should devote more attention to comparing and contrasting the merits of different types of convenience samples. After all, given the prevalence of convenience samples within developmental science, it behooves developmental scientists to minimize the disadvantages of convenience samples when it comes to generalizability. With respect to generalizability, we believe that homogeneous convenience samples as well as quota homogeneous convenience samples have key advantages over conventional conveniences samples and should be used more. To be clear, we are not advocating for the increased use of convenience samples within developmental science, as we believe the opposite and advocate that the use of probability samples within developmental science should increase. However, when researchers are limited to convenience samples, we advise adopting homogeneous convenience samples as a positive alternative to conventional convenience samples. Additionally, we are not advocating for the elimination of conventional convenience samples. Instead, we recommend that the current ratio of conventional to homogeneous convenience samples within developmental science, which is about 11 to 1 (Bornstein et al., 2013), is not optimal for our science and should be brought into balance. That said, given existing paradigms within developmental science, we see at least two obstacles to the increased adoption of homogeneous convenience samples.

The first may be a concern on the part of researchers that it could be difficult to obtain protocol approval by internal review boards (IRBs) or to secure external funding for homogeneous convenience samples. Many funding agencies require (or strongly recommend) inclusion of all major sociodemographic groups. For example, the National Institutes of Health released guidelines about including women and minorities in clinical research in 1994 (revised in 2001; NIH Office of Extramural Research, 2001) that indicate that all grant applications are evaluated for the inclusion of sociodemographic groups, and if groups are omitted, a strong justification is required. Although one way to avoid the potential ire of IRBs and funding agencies is to collect a heterogeneous convenience sample and then limit one's analyses to a homogeneous subsample (e.g., limit analyses to only European Americans), this approach has two key limitations. Aside from its inefficiency, it is only feasible for sociodemographic subgroups that are well-represented among the target population (and already well-represented within developmental research). For example, one could not collect a heterogeneous convenience sample and then limit the analyses to only Native Americans because, more than likely, the sample size of Native Americans would be far too small to examine on its own. Therefore, instead of collecting conventional or heterogeneous convenience samples and restricting analyses to a homogeneous subsample, we encourage researchers to make principled theoretical and statistical arguments to support their choices of better sampling strategies, even if the strategy proposed is homogeneous with respect to one or more sociodemographic groups. Researchers may be required to provide scientific and practical justification to IRBs and parents/community leaders to explain why certain groups are being excluded from study; some statistical justifications are provided herein. There also are specific steps that granting agencies and journal editors can take to encourage the use of homogeneous convenience samples. For example, granting agencies could set aside funds to support research using homogeneous convenience samples to study underrepresented (and understudied) subpopulations. Additionally, journal editors could organize special issues that are limited to studies that use homogeneous convenience samples to examine a specific substantive topic, say adolescent attachment, but vary as to the sociodemographic group of focus.

The second potential obstacle is developmental scientists' reticence to share data. In many cases, researchers hold exclusive rights to their data and tightly restrict access to their data, although this will become less of an obstacle over time, given that NIH now requires that all applications provide data sharing plans. However, for scientific knowledge to accumulate, researchers using homogeneous convenience samples will either have to share their data with other researchers or alternatively work collaboratively with other researchers in a manner that is not currently common. For example, returning to the six homogeneous convenience samples listed in Table 2b, to examine differences across ethnicity or SES directly, two or more of the six research teams would have to work together in one of two ways. At the point of data collection, they could coordinate their efforts so that they use the same measures and procedures and are, therefore, able to pool and analyze all data once collected. However, this level of coordination prior to data collection often proves challenging given varying priorities, time-tables, and resources across research teams. As another possibility, even if different research teams do not use the exact same measures, they could still integrate their data where possible post hoc using integrative data analysis (Curran & Hussong, 2009). Additionally, using meta-analysis, a single research team could examine whether a given effect size varies depending on a sample's sociodemographics. However, in many cases, this may prove difficult because developmental studies often do not provide detailed information regarding their sample's socio-demographics (see Bornstein et al., 2013).

Our core thesis is that because convenience samples of homogeneous populations (i.e., homogeneous convenience samples) are more likely to be representative than convenience samples of heterogeneous populations (i.e., conventional convenience samples), homogeneous convenience samples should, on average, yield more valid (less unbiased) estimates than conventional convenience samples. However, in terms of providing valid estimates, relative to homogeneous convenience samples, how much more disadvantaged are conventional convenience samples and how much more advantaged are probability samples? Moreover, are there specific conditions under which homogeneous convenience samples perform particularly better than conventional convenience samples (e.g., samples of smaller size or when multiple sociodemographic factors are homogeneous)? It is important for future research to address these issues both theoretically and statistically because the answers found will reveal exactly how much the field has to gain from the increased use of homogeneous convenience samples.

NOTES

1. When mean SES for the White adolescent population ($M^w = 0.2$) is applied to this equation, $\rho^w = 0.30$ (i.e., $0.30 = 0.280 + 0.100^* 0.2$), which is the population parameter for White adolescents.
2. When mean SES for the Black adolescent population ($M^b = -.8$) is applied to this equation, $\rho^b = 0.10$ (i.e., $0.10 = 0.128 + 0.035^* -.8$), which is the population parameter for Black adolescents.

REFERENCES

Bailey, J. A., Hill, K. G., Oesterle, S., & Hawkins, J. D. (2009). Parenting practices and problem behavior across three generations: Monitoring, harsh discipline, and drug use in the intergenerational transmission of externalizing behavior. *Developmental Psychology, 45* (5), 1214–1226.

Berlin, L. J., Ispa, J. M., Fine, M. A., Malone, P. S., Brooks-Gunn, J., Brady-Smith, C., et al. (2009). Correlates and consequences of spanking and verbal punishment for low-income White, African American, and Mexican American toddlers. *Child Development, 80*(5), 1403–1420.

Bettencourt, H., & Lopez, S. R. (1993). The study of culture, ethnicity, and race in American psychology. *American Psychologist, 48*, 629–637.

Bornstein, M. H., Jager, J., & Putnick, D. L. (2013). Sampling in developmental science: Situations, shortcomings, solutions, and standards. *Developmental Review, 33*, 357–370.

Burnette, M. L., Oshri, A., Lax, R., Richards, D., & Ragbeer, S. N. (2012). Pathways from harsh parenting to adolescent antisocial behavior: A multidomain test of gender moderation. *Development and Psychopathology, 24*, 857–870.

Cochran, W. G. (1977). *Sampling techniques.* (3rd ed.) New York, NY: Wiley.

Crimmins, E. M., & Saito, Y. (2001). Trends in health life expectancy in the United States, 1970-1990: Gender, racial, and educational differences. *Social Science and Medicine, 52*, 1629–1641.

Curran, P. J., & Hussong, A. M. (2009). Integrative data analysis: The simultaneous analysis of multiple data sets. *Psychological Methods, 14* (2), 81–100.

Davis-Kean, P. E., & Sexton, H. R. (2009). Race differences in parental influences on child achievement: Multiple pathways to success. *Merrill-Palmer Quarterly, 55* (3), 285–318.

Deater-Deckard, K., Dodge, K. A., Bates, J. E., & Pettit, G. S. (1996). Physical punishment among African American and European American mothers: Links to children's externalizing behaviors. *Developmental Psychology*, **32**, 1065–1072.

Desimone, L. (1999). Linking parent involvement with student achievement: Do race and income matter? *The Journal of Educational Research*, **93**, 11–30.

Faul, F., Erdfelder, E., Lang, A.-G., & Buchner, A. (2007). G*Power 3: A flexible statistical power analysis for the social, behavioral, and biomedical sciences. *Behavior Research Methods*, **39**, 175–191.

Geronimus, A. T., Bound, J., Keene, D., & Hicken, M. (2007). Black-white differences in age trajectories of hypertension prevalence among adult men and women, 1999–2002. *Ethnicity and Disease*, **17**, 40–48.

Gershoff, E. T., Lansford, J. E., Sexton, H. R., Davis-Kean, P., & Sameroff, A. J. (2012). Longitudinal links between spanking and children's externalizing behaviors in a national sample of White, Black, Hispanic, and Asian American Families. *Child Development*, **83** (3), 838–843.

Gunnoe, M. L., & Mariner, C. L. (1997). Toward a developmental-contextual model of the effects of parental spanking on children's aggression. *Archives of Pediatric and Adolescent Medicine*, **151**, 768–775.

Jager, J. (2011). A developmental shift in Black-White differences in depressive affect across adolescence and early adulthood: The influence of early adult social roles and socio-economic status. *International Journal of Behavioral Development*, **35** (5), 457–469.

Jager, J., & Davis-Kean, P. E. (2011). Same-sex sexuality and adolescent psychological well-being: The influence of sexual orientation, early reports of same-sex attraction, and gender. *Self and Identity*, **10** (4), 417–444.

Kessler, R. C., & Neighbors, H. W. (1986). A new perspective on the relationships among race, social class, and psychological distress. *Journal of Health and Social Behavior*, **27**, 107–115.

Lansford, J. E., Deater-Deckard, K., Dodge, K. A., Bates, J., & Pettit, G. S. (2004). Ethnic differences in the link between physical discipline and later adolescent externalizing behaviors. *Journal of Child Psychology and Psychiatry*, **45**, 801–812.

Levy, P. S., & Lemeshow, S. (2011). *Sampling of populations: Methods and applications* (4th ed.). New York, NY: Wiley.

Mays, V. M., Ponce, N. A., Washington, D. L., & Cochran, S. D. (2003). Classification of race and ethnicity: Implications for Public Health. *Annual Review of Public Health*, **24**, 83–110.

McLoyd, V. C., & Smith, J. (2002). Physical discipline and behavior problems in African American, European American, and Hispanic Children: Emotional support as a moderator. *Journal of Marriage and Family*, **64**, 40–53.

National Institutes of Health. Office of Extramural Research. (2001). *NIH Policy and Guidelines on The Inclusion of Women and Minorities as Subjects in Clinical Research—Amended, October, 2001*. Available online: http://grants.nih.gov/grants/funding/women_min/guideli nes_amended_10_2001.htm

Phinney, J. S. (1996). When we talk about American ethnic groups, what do we mean? *American Psychologist*, **51**, 918–927.

Rothbaum, F., & Weisz, J. R. (1994). Parental caregiving and child externalizing behavior in nonclinical samples: A meta-analysis. *Psychological Bulletin*, **116** (1), 55–74.

U.S. Census Bureau. (2012). *Current Population Survey, Annual Social and Economic Supplement, 2011*. Washington, DC: Author.

III. FROM SMALL TO BIG: METHODS FOR INCORPORATING LARGE SCALE DATA INTO DEVELOPMENTAL SCIENCE

Pamela E. Davis-Kean and Justin Jager

This article is part of the issue "Developmental Methodology" Card (Issue Author). For a full listing of articles in this issue, see: http://onlinelibrary.wiley.com/doi/10.1111/mono.v82.2/issuetoc.

For decades, developmental science has been based primarily on relatively small-scale data collections with children and families. Part of the reason for the dominance of this type of data collection is the complexity of collecting cognitive and social data on infants and small children. These small data sets are limited in both power to detect differences and the demographic diversity to generalize clearly and broadly. Thus, in this chapter we will discuss the value of using existing large-scale data sets to tests the complex questions of child development and how to develop future large-scale data sets that are both representative and can answer the important questions of developmental scientists.

FROM SMALL TO BIG: USING LARGE SCALE DATA SETS IN DEVELOPMENTAL SCIENCE

Developmental psychology, like many of the psychology fields, aims to illuminate the human condition by understanding the role that individuals play in influencing their own behavior as well as the behavior of others. However, specific to developmental science is the role that age and time play

Corresponding author: Pamela E. Davis-Kean, University of Michigan, Ann Arbor, MI; email:pdakean@umich.edu

This paper was supported by grants to the first author from the National Science Foundation for the NSF-supported Collaboration for the Analysis of Pathways from Childhood to Adulthood grant numbers 0322356 and 0818478. The opinions are those of the authors and do not necessarily reflect those of the National Science Foundation.

DOI: 10.1111/mono.12297

in understanding the psychological outcomes of the individual. Developmentalists track individuals across age and time to understand the stability or change in a psychological construct or behavior that may be of interest or concern to society (e.g., mental health, physical health, achievement). This focus on age and time has put developmental psychology, and more broadly developmental science, in the position of observing individuals at multiple time points across the lifespan. Historically, we made these observations by using experimental methods on cross-sections of children at different ages (e.g., Piaget & Inhelder, 1966) where comparisons were made between age groups of children. Our statistical methods were rather rudimentary and did not allow for the examination of how individual children develop and change across time (i.e., within-person comparison), rendering it difficult to ascertain or discuss how the same child looked at age 5 and age 12. Fortunately, developmental methodology has changed quite dramatically in the last few years and now we have powerful statistical methods for examining change across time and across individuals (Laursen, Little, & Card, 2012). Thus, we can now discuss commonalities across children of different ages but also the individual development of children across multiple ages.

The advances in statistical methods, however, have not led to similar advances in how developmental data are collected or used to understand the complexity of child development. Instead, as Jager et al. (Chapter 2, this volume) discuss in detail, much of research data on child development is still collected on relatively small, convenience samples and is not generalizable or representative of the broad population (Henrich, Heine, & Norenzayan, 2010; Jager et al., Chapter 2, this volume). One reason developmental data are still often collected in this manner is that the types of data that are used to study children and their families is complex, and there are real barriers to collecting data based on, for example, diagnostic tests or home observations, at a larger scale. However, more recent sampling methods would allow for this complexity in larger and more representative samples (Davis-Kean & Jager, 2012). Indeed, as we will describe, large-scale data sets provide more power to address the often subtler questions of child development and thus lead to a fuller understanding of development or change across time.

To be clear, we are not arguing or suggesting that large-scale data sets are the only valid method for studying development. Instead, we posit that there are important advantages to the use of large-scale, longitudinal data for furthering the study of development. For example, we agree with Jager et al. (Chapter 2, this volume) that the use of "homogeneous" convenience samples in the place of "conventional" convenience samples can limit the diminished generalizability associated with the use of small-scale data or convenience samples. Moreover, we also agree with Jager et al. (Chapter 2, this volume) that the use of large-scale data, including "probability" samples, within developmental science should increase.

Hence, in this chapter we will discuss the value of using large-scale data sets to test the complex questions of child development. We will begin with an overview of the relative advantages of cross-sectional and longitudinal data, considering also the challenges of each with small data sets. We will also describe the importance of representative samples when studying children and families, and the challenges toward this goal posed by small data sets. We will describe the advantages of large-scale data sets, as well as methods for using a combination of small and large-scale data sets to validate results across multiple studies. We will end with steps to consider for collecting new large-scale data sets or obtaining existing large-scale data sets that are useful for answering important developmental questions.

ADVANTAGES AND DISADVANTAGES OF CROSS-SECTIONAL AND LONGITUDINAL DATA

Cross-Sectional Data

When considering children's language acquisition, theory of mind development, attachment to parent, executive function development, and many other developmental outcomes in children, developmental scientists have used inter-individual change designs to understand age differences (Ainsworth, 1979; Wellman, Cross, & Watson, 2001; Zelazo, Frye, & Rapus, 1996). In these classic methods, children are recruited at various ages and administered assessments. Differences are then examined across age cohorts to determine if there are age-related changes in the phenomenon under study. Some of the most famous of these types of age-cohort experiments were conducted by Piaget and his coworkers (e.g., Piaget & Inhelder, 1966) and for years defined the study of cognitive development. There are many advantages to this method with perhaps the strongest being the relatively short time period needed for collecting data across a potentially large age range. Thus, collecting data from multiple ages has historically been used to examine and discuss age changes within a single cross-sectional data collection and, thereby, disseminate the findings of their research relatively quickly. Many of the age-related theories that are seminal works in developmental science have used this type of method to understand development. There are, however, issues with relying on cross-sectional methods for the study of development.

As suggested earlier, a major limitation to the cross-sectional method is the inability to examine intra-individual change or how individual children change across time on multiple outcomes. Using attachment research as an illustrative example, one may want to see how an individual child changes in attachment strategies with the parents across infancy to early childhood. This intra-individual change would answer the question of whether or not children exhibit the same attachment style across time or as they develop. If a child is labeled securely attached at infancy and we base our research findings on the correlates or manipulations at that time point, then we may miss that this attachment style was only true for this child at this time point of development or even on the day of testing, but not true for later points of development (see Rush & Hofer, Chapter 5, this volume). Thus, collecting additional time points on the individual child and family may lead to important nuances in attachment theory and help us understand how contextual changes (e.g., entry into child care or schooling) may relate to changes in parent–child attachment. The additional data also allows for a deeper understanding of the actual *development* of this phenomena and not just the existence of the phenomena in child development (Ornstein & Haden, 2001).

Longitudinal Data

Like cross-sectional data, longitudinal data have limitations. The majority of longitudinal data are correlational rather than experimental and therefore ill-suited to examine causality. One can create experimental conditions for longitudinal data (e.g., Abecedarian Project; Campbell et al., 2008) but any biased attrition (same type of group disproportionately leaving the study) or control contagion (seeking out the services that the experimental groups are receiving) can call into question the findings of the study. Longitudinal researchers also must deal with the reliability of their measurement across time and whether the same measure is appropriate across distinct periods of development (i.e., is the measure equally appropriate for 4-year-olds and 10-year-olds; see Grimm et al., Chapter 4, this volume). Indeed, one of the challenges that longitudinal researchers face is how to create measures of constructs that are valid across age groups. Statistically, we are able to test equivalence of measures across time, but that is a post hoc way of correcting for lack of validity in the measure (Meredith & Horn, 2001). It would be more advantageous for developmental science to have a group of measurements that are validated across time and with known functional forms of development. Understanding what the "norm" of a phenomenon may be at any age allows us to make inferences on whether the outcome is following a normative developmental trajectory or is deviating in important ways from the average change. For example, the longitudinal work on achievement now gives us some idea of the functional forms across schooling (Davis-Kean & Jager, 2014; Murnane et al., 2006; Reardon & Robinson, 2008), recent work by Jager, Schulenberg, O'Malley, and Bachman (2013) and Jager, Keyes, and Schulenberg (2015) has laid the groundwork for understanding historical variation in the functional form of substance use during adolescence and the transition to adulthood, and functional forms of the subscales of problems behaviors are now useful in understanding the normative changes of behavior across time (Olson et al., 2013).

34

Sampling and Sample Size

Although longitudinal data can help inform some of these important developmental changes, it does not overcome two of the persistent problems of developmental science: (1) the lack of representative samples (e.g., demographic composition of the sample does not align with the demographic composition of the larger target population), and (2) the overreliance on small samples (Henrich et al., 2010; Kraemer, Yesavage, Taylor, & Kupfer, 2000). There have been some well-designed developmental studies at the population level (e.g., the Early Childhood Longitudinal Study-Birth Cohort; ECLS-B), but much of the research in developmental science still relies on convenience samples that are comprised of children and families who are in small areas surrounding the university and willing to participate. Other studies are done in more diverse locations like Head Start Centers, but again, these studies represent the more circumscribed population that happens to be available in that context (see Jager et al., Chapter 2, this volume, on ways to use this homogeneity as an advantage). Although generalizability from these studies is unclear, the findings nonetheless are often broadly generalized and discussed as common to all developing children.

In addition to unclear generalizability, convenience samples are also often small and lack sufficient statistical power to answer a researcher's questions. As is often the case with developmental research, we are recruiting from the community institutions such as judicial systems, medical settings, and schools. This recruitment is based on putting advertisements in local papers, child care centers, university hallways, and anywhere else that children and families may be recruited. Though these methods of recruitment are an attempt to increase the sample size of the studies, they still often result in samples that are small and lack the diversity or population representation to produce clearly generalizable results (Bornstein, Jager, & Putnick, 2013; Campbell & Stanley, 1963; Cohen & Cohen, 1984).

To address these problems, researchers can help to broaden the generalizability of their study at the design phase, if they elect to sample systematically and sufficiently across diverse groups (e.g., sex, race, country of origin). Additionally, the issue of poor statistical power can be mitigated, if not altogether avoided, when designing the study, if researchers have a firm understanding of how statistical power relates to the number of participants sampled. Both cross-sectional and longitudinal developmental data share these design problems and both problems are important to consider and resolve if we are to increase the robustness of developmental science.

Are there ways that developmental researchers can enhance their studies in order to address the issue of sample size and generalizability? The next section will address this issue by discussing how large-scale data sets can be used to address developmental questions and how researchers can use these data sets to validate cross-sectional findings as well as extend these findings across development without having to collect time-intensive longitudinal data.

As noted earlier, the statistical methods available to developmental scientists have greatly expanded (Laursen et al., 2012). This expansion has led to a relatively new and exciting field of developmental methodology where questions of how individuals change across time and across context are now readily assessed and tested. Advances in longitudinal design have also helped to ease some of the burdens of longitudinal data collection (i.e., expense and time) while also increasing the rigor of developmental research. These advances include the use of accelerated longitudinal designs (Duncan & Duncan, 2012), planned-missingness designs (Graham, Taylor, Olchowski, & Cumsille, 2006), and regression discontinuity designs (Ludwig & Miller, 2007). In this section, we propose another option that can be used by developmental researchers to answer their questions: large-scale longitudinal data. In this case, "large-scale" developmental data means a data set that has broad or expansive research applications. These types of data sets need not be nationally representative samples (or "probability" samples to use the nomenclature of Jager et al., Chapter 2, this volume). However, in order to serve as a rich source of data for answering developmental questions, these data sets do need to be large in terms of sample size, diverse in terms of demographics, and ideally broad in terms of measurement.

One promising application of large-scale data is the incorporation of multiple secondary, large-scale data sources for answering important developmental questions. For example, Duncan et al. (2007) used six large-scale, longitudinal data sets from multiple countries to examine the role of early skills in reading, math, and attention on outcomes at entry to school. Prior to this article, there were multiple studies that suggested that social skills or behavior problems were just as important as academic skills in predicting to success in schooling. This article used the strength of large-scale, national, longitudinal data sets like the National Longitudinal Study of Youth (NLSY) and the Early Childhood Longitudinal Study (ECLS-K) and the British Cohort Studies (BSS) as well as large-scale, community longitudinal samples such as the NICHD Study of Early Child Care and Youth Development (NICHD-SECCYD), the Infant Health and Development Program (IHDP), and the Montreal Longitudinal Experimental Preschool Study (MLEPS) to explore which early skills where predictive of later school readiness success. Combining the population data sets that were less precise in the measurement of the developmental phenomena with the community samples that had stronger measurement properties but were less diverse in representing the population (see Davis-Kean & Jager, 2012, for review of these issues and a table of data sets that are available), allowed for a robust test of the question about early skills and school readiness. The findings were somewhat surprising in that they found that math skills were the strongest predictor of early school success followed by reading and attention skills, but not behavior problems or social skills, which were largely unrelated. By using the power of replication, this article was able to show, perhaps not so surprisingly, that students need basic math and reading skills to achieve in schools. An important additional contribution was the importance of attention skills in early schooling. Moreover, this article suggests that future research should explore the development of these early skills as well as their potential for school-based interventions.

Whereas Duncan et al. (2007) used multiple, secondary longitudinal data sets as a way to validate and test the effects of important psychological variables, Davis-Kean and colleagues (2008) used multiple secondary longitudinal data sets to understand discontinuity in developmental linkages beliefs about the self. Specifically, Davis-Kean and colleagues (2008) examined the relation between self-efficacy beliefs and actual outcomes (achievement and aggression) in children across development. To do so, they used two secondary, large-scale longitudinal data sets. The question addressed was whether young children can provide reliable and valid data for predicting important outcomes (achievement and aggression) from their self-beliefs across development, an important question given years of research that had been collecting self-efficacy data on children as young as 4 and 5 years of age. In pursuit of their question, Davis-Kean et al. (2008) were able to replicate their findings across multiple data sets and across different self-efficacy beliefs. The results indicated that children's self-efficacy beliefs of achievement and aggression prior to 8–10 years of age did not reliably predict the outcomes considered. Instead, there seems to be a gradual increase in the relations across time, with early adolescents and adolescence showing the strongest relations between beliefs and behaviors. This research provides evidence for a cognitive-developmental change in how children think about themselves in relation to their own behaviors (Davis-Kean, Jager, & Collins, 2009). It also allows researchers to consider the most useful time to measure these beliefs via self-reports if the goal is predicting behavior. Because these findings were replicated across multiple data sets, there is stronger evidence that this phenomenon is robust and that theories supporting early belief-behavior connections may need to be modified to take into account changes in cognitive development and the understanding of the self (Davis-Kean et al., 2009).

How does the use of large-scale data in conjunction with other data benefit developmental scientists who collect their own small-scale data in laboratory settings or collect cross-sectional age-cohort studies? In short, these researchers can use large-scale data to validate and replicate findings they obtain from their own primary data. As was highlighted earlier, large-scale data collections often have large sample sizes of children and families, are diverse in race and socioeconomic status, and contain a diverse set of variables that can be used to understand selection effects (Davis-Kean & Jager, 2012). Again, using attachment as an illustrative example, imagine if attachment was examined among a small-scale convenience sample of mostly low-income children and the laboratory-based strange situation task (Ainsworth, 1979) was used to determine the attachment style of the child. In this hypothetical example, the researcher may question whether the findings were generalizable to all low-income children or just the ones that were recruited and were willing to come to the laboratory for testing. Also, there are other potential problems with the sample's composition that bring generalizability further into question: (1) the study recruited participants for 3 months but were only able to obtain 30 mother–child dyads, (2) far more dyads included daughters than sons, and (3) not all of the dyads had mothers who were low income. However, despite these multiple issues, the data are very rich in understanding the issue of attachment. Once the data are analyzed, only a few of the children are found to be securely attached and those that are securely attached are the children with mothers with the lowest income. Because these findings are contrary to what others have found in the literature, this study's novel findings could potentially change the way attachment is characterized as related to lower socioeconomic families.

However, as noted throughout this example, there are many reasons to question whether and to whom these results generalize and whether the unique demographic composition of the convenience sample itself is what is driving the results. This situation is where the use of a large-scale data set can help validate the research and also make a stronger contribution to developmental science. The NICHD-SECCYD data set has data on attachment from approximately 1,300 children around the United States and is easily available to researchers. Returning to our hypothetical example, the researcher could isolate the same age cohort and income levels used in the small study to replicate the analyses in a much larger and more diverse data set. Not only can the research question be validated, but the researcher now has other variables that can be used to further explain the phenomenon that was found. It may be that the families from the lowest incomes were overrepresented by students who were working on higher degrees. So, the finding may be related to parental education and not to income status. Multiple other alternative hypotheses can be tested, but the most important question is whether the research from the lab was validated. If it was not, and if the spurious finding was published, then the incorrect conclusion and the generalization to other low-income families would be in the research literature (see also Card, Chapter 7, this volume, for further consideration of the importance of replication). Although in this example the longitudinal nature of the NICHD-SECCYD data set was not utilized, it certainly could have been by specifying attachment as a predictor of future outcomes or by examining change in attachment over time.

CREATING LARGE-SCALE DATA SETS FOR DEVELOPMENTAL RESEARCHERS

Many developmental scientists are unaware of the availability of population and large-scale longitudinal data sets for use in their own research. Many questions that are being answered with small-scale primary data collection can be answered in these larger data sets and in the case of the population data sets, much more representative samples than are available in the small-scale primary data. Information on how to obtain these data sets and the types of developmental questions that can be answered using these resources is available in a publication by Davis-Kean and Jager (2012). We will not reiterate that discussion here, but instead turn our attention to what is missing from those available large-scale data sets that might be useful for developmental scientists.

With the exception of the NICHD-SECCYD, the majority of the national, population studies were not designed by developmental scientists for the sake of child development research. Instead, they were designed by other social scientists for examining families or education systems. Often, the psychological measures used in these data sets are truncated versions of inventories and diagnostic tests that have been published in the literature. These compromises in measurement, typically made in order to fit the question to the data set, are often not optimal for understanding the phenomenon of interest to developmental scientists. Although there are longitudinal data sets that are available at various archives (e.g., Murray Center, www.murray. harvard.edu; ICPSR.www.icpsr.umich.edu) that were designed by developmental scientists/psychologists, many of these relate to the specific theory or model of the primary investigator and, therefore, do not contain the breadth of measures needed to answer broader or more diverse developmental questions.

Thus, most large-scale data sets have inadequate measurement of psychological constructs, and those large-scale data sets that are designed by psychologists are often narrow in scope and, therefore, have limited applicability. This limitation of existing large-scale data sets points to the need for the creation of new developmental data sets that are designed to address questions and constructs that are common in developmental science, have sufficiently large and representative samples of not only the target population but also demographic subpopulations (e.g., race, gender, and SES subgroups), and can easily be archived and accessed by researchers (secured but not proprietary).

One way to promote these types of data sets is to form consortia or collaborations of developmental scientists to create a data set that can be used by a wide group of developmental researchers to answer questions important to the field. This type of collaboration has been done previously in the case of the NICHD-SECCYD, and many Head Start research and evaluation efforts involve consortia of researchers designing the studies. Thus, there is a precedence for these type of efforts. However, these data sets are often not representative of the population, and those that are representative and not designed by developmental scientists (e.g., ECLS-Kindergarten & Birth cohorts) do not have the type of developmental measures that are commonly used by developmental researchers. These data sets often omit longitudinal measures of executive function, theory of mind, attachment, mental health diagnoses, intelligence, language acquisition, disabilities and special needs, early motor and cognitive skills, early play and peer interactions, and parent–child interactions. The lack of important developmental measures crosses the domains of both social and cognitive development, with many cognitive development measures being mostly ignored in large-scale data collection. It is the case that including all of the scales and assessments of the important variables of interest to development may be too time-consuming and it may be unethical to ask caregivers and children to devote the time to completing such a complex array of measures. There are certainly issues with participant burden and, indeed, university internal review boards (IRBs) may not approve the hours of interviewing needed to obtain this data for a family, but, as we discuss below, there are developmental methods available to reduce these burdens.

The question at hand is how to go about conceiving and constructing a new large-scale data set that does not share the limitations of existing ones. First, one would need the assistance of a good sampling design researcher or organization that can help in designing ways to obtain a diverse population sample. There are multiple organizations across the United States that have this expertise, often found associated with Population Research Centers. After a sample and appropriate sample size has been determined (based on anticipated effect size), then the issue is how often and what measures should be used. Many of the available longitudinal data sets consist of yearly measurement occasions; however, many constructs that are studied, like regulation and achievement, may develop over a shorter time span, especially for young children. Thus, important transitions may be missed, and the stability in various psychological characteristics over a 1-year period may be the wrong time frame to examine. For some measures there may be sufficient stability to warrant assessments that are no more frequent than once a year, but there is little empirical work that has provided the normative functional forms of our measures so that we would be able to make these decisions. Thus, decisions need to be made about the frequency of measurements at different ages in order to fully capture the phenomenon of interests.

The next task is to design the study in such a way as to reduce the amount of time that our participants are interacting with research staff. Combining designs such as accelerated-longitudinal designs (Miyazaki & Raudenbush, 2000) (multiple age cohorts) with planned missingness designs (Rush &

Hofer, Chapter 5, this volume), in which a small common group of items can recover a full inventory, can reduce the time that participants are being interviewed or completing questionnaires. These sorts of designs also provide researchers with longitudinal data on multiple age cohorts of children. Technology can also be used to reduce the burden of interviewing by providing questionnaires via computer, smartphone, or other digital devices. Additionally, measurement that has traditionally been performed in laboratories can be adapted to these technologies. Questions regarding thoughts and feelings can be accessed through beeper studies (Prescott & Csikszentmihalyi, 1981) and texting and visual coding of the home environment can be done through smartphone videotaping. If these data are collected throughout a day, week, or month, which can be done with these devices, then we have repeated measures of a phenomenon that may be sufficiently sensitive to developmental change (emotions, language acquisition). This type of data collection also creates "big data" such that we have multiple measures of a phenomenon across multiple time periods allowing for a complex systems approach to the analysis of developmental data. With these sorts of data we would also be able to better disentangle transactional models (Sameroff, 2009), which to date have mostly only been tested across years as opposed to moments to determine if a child instigates a parental behavior or the parent instigates a child behavior. At the moment, the data used to test these models are not sensitive to the actual transaction but more so to the stability of the transactions.

Though we have provided a roadmap for how a new large-scale data collection could be designed to benefit the developmental community, there are still many obstacles to overcome. Researchers are often concerned about putting effort into such a data collection and then allowing others to benefit from that effort. Our colleagues in the sociological and economics fields have already provided some of the groundwork for the collaborative use of large-scale data sets. In the case of these social sciences, data sets are collected by an individual or group for the benefit of the larger scientific community. These data sets are intended to be used by researchers and students to answer a broad array of questions that are important to the field of study. The important aspect is that data are collected on as many relevant areas of the science as possible at the time that the study is designed. The data are not proprietary data with the understanding that the breadth of the data set lends itself to answering many questions and taking different approaches to data. This type of data collection, where the focus is on the field of study instead of individual questions, would increase the quality of data available as well as our ability to validate and replicate our science, which ultimately would strengthen our science and the applicability of what we do for the constituents of our science: children and families. It also would provide a training ground for students and post-doctoral fellows to learn more sophisticated developmental methods and statistics as has occurred in the other social sciences.

Most importantly, we could better examine subgroups of interest to developmental scientists with data that represents their population instead of making comparisons between groups that are different in more than just the grouping variable being used (e.g., sex, race). Thus, we are at a point that the developmental science community can validate and strengthen our research findings and create new data sources that may lead to new research opportunities in the future.

SUMMARY AND DISCUSSION

Scientists should use all the tools that are available to them in order to validate the phenomena under study. Often, however, scientists become accustomed or trained on one type of method and use it exclusively to answer their questions. Equally common is that strong arguments are made about the superiority of one method over the other (e.g., cross-sectional or longitudinal). As we reviewed here, there are advantages and disadvantages to various methods, and in the end our goal is to create the strongest and highest quality science that is possible. In particular, we believe that the expanded use of large-scale and representative developmental data is one important way to broaden our knowledge of development. One avenue for expansion entails the use of existing large-scale data sets either in conjunction with one another to garner authoritative accounts of developmental trends, or in conjunction with primary data to validate findings from smaller-scale convenience studies. Another avenue for expansion entails the creation of new large-scale data sets developed by developmental scientists to address a broad array of developmental questions.

The ability to use multiple large-scale data sets to verify existing research findings is new to developmental methods and may be an important avenue for strengthening developmental research in the future. It allows researchers to go from small convenience studies to larger, more representative studies. This in turn expands research questions into important domains, such as how cognitive development interacts with contextual changes across time to predict to outcomes in children. Even though these techniques are not yet widely used, we believe that developmental science is well situated to take advantage of using multiple modes of data collection to validate and expand its findings. The use of large-scale data sets to replicate developmental research findings is a powerful addition to the methodological toolbox of developmental scientists and it is, in general, easily obtainable from data archives or from the research institutions that have collected the data. Currently, some granting agencies require plans for data archiving and dissemination of data that are collected with federal monies, and this requirement may lead to an even richer collection of data sets that can be used for validating and replicating developmental findings.

Relative to the expanded use of existing large-scale data sets, the creation of new large-scale developmental data sets may prove more of a challenge. Psychological constructs typically require in-depth measurement (i.e., measures that are time intensive, observational, and/or consist of many items). In contrast, a hallmark of large-scale data are the breadth of measures (many different constructs are measured) at the expense of depth of measurement (Davis-Kean & Jager, 2012). Thus, when designing and creating large-scale developmental data sets with broad psychological application, developmental scientists will have to balance their desire for depth of measurement against the need for breadth of measures. Of course, this is no easy task, as it will require cooperation among different research teams competing to make sure their areas of study are properly (and fully) measured. Given these limitations, however, it is clear that the data quality, validity, and relevance to important constituent groups of our research are within our grasp. It is hoped that applying some new ideas to developmental methods will help improve the science and, perhaps most importantly, help us find the answers to complex developmental questions in the future.

REFERENCES

Ainsworth, M. S. (1979). Infant-mother attachment. *American Psychologist*, **34**(10), 932.

Bornstein, M. H., Jager J., & Putnick, D. L. (2013). Sampling in developmental science: Situations, shortcomings, solutions, and standards. *Developmental Review*, **33**, 357–370.

Campbell, D. T., & Stanley, J. C. (1963). *Experimental and quasi-experimental designs for research.* Boston, MA: Houghton Mifflin.

Campbell, F. A., Wasik, B. H., Burchinal, M., Barbarin, O., Kainz, K., Sparling, J. J., et al. (2008). Young adult outcomes of the Abecedarian and CARE early childhood educational interventions. *Early Childhood Research Quarterly*, **23**, 452–466.

Cohen, P., & Cohen, J. (1984). The clinician's illusion. *Archives of General Psychiatry*, **41**(12), 1178–1182.

Davis-Kean, P. E., Huesmann, R., Jager, J., Collins, A., Bates, J., & Lansford, J. (2008). Changes in the relation of beliefs and behaviors across development. *Child Development*, **79**(5), 1257–1269.

Davis-Kean, P. E., & Jager, J. (2012). The use of large-scale data sets for the study of developmental science. In B. Laursen, T. Little, & A. Card (Eds.), *Handbook of developmental research methods* (pp. 148–162). New York, NY: Guilford Press.

Davis-Kean, P. E., & Jager, J. (2014). Trajectories of achievement within race/ethnicity: "Catching up" in achievement across time. *Journal of Educational Research*, **107**(3): 197–208.

Davis-Kean, P. E., Jager, J., & Collins, W. A. (2009). The self in action: An emerging link between self-beliefs and behaviors in middle childhood. *Child Development Perspectives*, **3**(3), 184–188.

Duncan, G. J., Dowsett, C. J., Claessens, A., Magnuson, K., Huston, A. C., Klebanov, P., et al. (2007). School readiness and later achievement. *Developmental Psychology*, 43(6), 1428–1446.

Duncan, S. C., & Duncan, T. E. (2012). Accelerated longitudinal designs. In B. Laursen, T. Little, & A. Card (Eds.), *Handbook of developmental research methods* (pp. 31–45). New York, NY: Guilford Press.

Graham, J. W., Taylor, B. J., Olchowski, A. E., & Cumsille, P. E. (2006). Planned missing data designs in psychological research. *Psychological Methods*, 11(4), 323–343.

Henrich, J., Heine, S. J., & Norenzayan, A. (2010). The weirdest people in the world? *Behavioral and Brain Sciences*, 33(2–3), 61–83.

Jager, J., Keyes, K. M., & Schulenberg, J. E. (2015). Historical variation in young adult binge drinking trajectories and its link to historical variation in social roles and minimum legal drinking age. *Developmental Psychology*, 51(7), 962–974.

Jager, J., Schulenberg, J. E., O'Malley, P. M., & Bachman, J. G. (2013). Historical variation in drug use trajectories across the transition to adulthood: The trend towards lower intercepts and steeper, ascending slopes. *Development and Psychopathology*, 25(2), 527–543.

Kraemer, H. C., Yesavage, J. A., Taylor, J. L., & Kupfer, D. (2000). How can we learn about developmental processes from cross-sectional studies, or can we? *American Journal of Psychiatry*, 157(2), 163–171.

Laursen, B., Little, T. D., & Card, N. A. (2012). *Handbook of developmental research methods*. New York, NY: Guilford Press.

Ludwig, J., & Miller, D. L. (2007). Does head start improve children's life chances? Evidence from a regression discontinuity design. *The Quarterly Journal of Economics*, 122(1), 159–208.

Meredith, W. & Horn, J. (2001). The role of factorial invariance in modeling growth and change. In L. M. Collins & A. G. Sayer (Eds.), *New methods for the analysis of change: Decade of behavior* (pp. 203–240). Washington, DC: American Psychological Association, xxiv, 442 pp. http://doi.org/10.1037/10409-007

Miyazaki, Y., & Raudenbush, S. W. (2000). Tests for linkage of multiple cohorts in an accelerated longitudinal design. *Psychological Methods*, 5(1), 44.

Murnane, R. J., Willett, J. B., Bub, K. L., McCartney, K., Hanushek, E., & Maynard, R. (2006). Understanding Trends in the Black-White Achievement Gaps during the First Years of School [with Comments]. *Brookings-Wharton papers on urban affairs* (pp. 197–135). Washington, DC: Brookings Institute Press.

Olson, S. L., Sameroff, A. J., Lansford, J. E., Sexton, H., Davis-Kean, P., Bates, J. E., et al. (2013). Deconstructing the externalizing spectrum: Growth patterns of overt aggression, covert aggression, oppositional behavior, impulsivity/inattention, and emotion dysregulation between school entry and early adolescence. *Development and Psychopathology*, 25(03), 817–842.

Ornstein, P. A., & Haden, C. A. (2001). Memory development or the development of memory? *Current Directions in Psychological Science*, 10(6), 202–205.

Piaget, J., & Inhelder, B. (1966). *The psychology of the child*. Paris: University of France Press.

Prescott, S., & Csikszentmihalyi, M. (1981). Environmental effects on cognitive and affective states: The experiential time sampling approach. *Social Behavior and Personality: An International Journal*, 9(1), 23–32.

Reardon, S. F., & Robinson, J. P. (2008). Patterns and trends in racial/ethnic and socioeconomic academic achievement gaps. In Helen F. Ladd & Edward B. Fiske (Eds.), *Handbook of research in education finance and policy*. (pp. 499–518). New York: Routledge.

Sameroff, A. J. (2009). *The transactional model of development: How children and contexts shape each other.* Washington, DC: American Psychological Association. http://doi.org/10.1037/11877-000

Wellman, H. M., Cross, D., & Watson, J. (2001). Meta-analysis of theory-of-mind development: The truth about false belief. *Child Development, 72*(3), 655–684.

Zelazo, P. D., Frye, D., & Rapus, T. (1996). An age-related dissociation between knowing rules and using them. *Cognitive Development, 11*(1), 37–63.

IV. DEVELOPMENTS IN THE ANALYSIS OF LONGITUDINAL DATA

Kevin J. Grimm, Pega Davoudzadeh, and Nilam Ram

This article is part of the issue "Developmental Methodology" Card (Issue Author). For a full listing of articles in this issue, see: http://onlinelibrary.wiley.com/doi/10.1111/mono.v82.2/issuetoc.

Longitudinal data analytic techniques include a complex array of statistical techniques from repeated-measures analysis of variance, mixed-effects models, and time-series analysis, to longitudinal latent variable models (e.g., growth models, dynamic factor models) and mixture models (longitudinal latent profile analysis, growth mixture models). In this article, we focus our attention on the rationales of longitudinal research laid out by Baltes and Nesselroade (1979) and discuss the advancements in the analysis of longitudinal data since their landmark paper. We highlight the developments in growth and change analysis and its derivatives because these models best capture the rationales for conducting longitudinal research. We conclude with additional rationales of longitudinal research brought about by the development of new analytic techniques.

Longitudinal data analysis encompasses and informs a wide range of theory, goals, methods, measurement paradigms, models, statistical frameworks, data configurations (e.g., data incompleteness, panel data, individually varying measurements), and historical debates and controversies. To organize a discussion on this topic, we first provide a brief overview of longitudinal data.

Corresponding author: Kevin J. Grimm, Ph.D., Professor, Department of Psychology, Arizona State University, PO Box 871104, Tempe, AZ 85287-1104; email: kjgrimm@asu.edu

The authors would like to thank Jack McArdle, John Nesselroade, Keith Widaman, the Quantitative and Developmental Methodology Lab at the University of California, Davis, and the Health and Developmental Research Methods Lab at Arizona State University.
DOI: 10.1111/mono.12298

We then look back at the work of Baltes and Nesselroade, who, in 1979, presented a series of rationales for conducting longitudinal research (Baltes & Nesselroade, 1979). The five rationales discussed by Baltes and Nesselroade are, in essence, opportunities that longitudinal data afforded researchers that cross-sectional data did not. Thus, these were opportunities made possible by repeatedly collecting data on the same individual, group of individuals, or groups of individuals over time. These rationales provide a useful scheme for organizing both longitudinal data analytic techniques (see McArdle & Nesselroade, 2014) and substantive inquiry into particular developmental phenomena (see Gerstorf & Ram, 2013).

Subsequently, we describe an array of longitudinal methods that have been developed since the publication of Baltes and Nesselroade's rationales. These methods have brought these rationales to the forefront of applied developmental research and have, in turn, highlighted additional opportunities of inquiry when conducting longitudinal research. We conclude with some remarks about what the future of longitudinal data and methods hold.

LONGITUDINAL DATA

To seed this discussion, we first briefly describe some special features inherent to longitudinal data. By definition longitudinal data are obtained when the same entity (e.g., individual, dyad, and/or group) is measured repeatedly at known points in time (see Dearborn & Rothney, 1941; known points in time may simply represent a known ordering of observations or the exact time of the measurement relative to a specific event, such as birth, death, marriage, beginning of study, etc.). Longitudinal data can be obtained on any time scale, both across (e.g., yearly surveys) and within measurement occasion (e.g., multiple trials on a task or multiple items on a test; see Bowles, 2006). In longitudinal research, the same variables or constructs are often measured over time, but we do not see this as one of the key features of longitudinal data; however, it is often seen as an important feature of repeated-measures data.

BALTES AND NESSELROADE'S RATIONALES FOR LONGITUDINAL RESEARCH

Summarizing the dialectic surrounding lifespan development in the 1970s, Baltes and Nesselroade (1979) presented five rationales for conducting longitudinal research, which are briefly summarized in Table 1. Still very much relevant today, these rationales outline the primary motivations for most developmentally oriented inquiries. The first rationale and primary reason for conducting longitudinal research is the *Direct Identification of*

TABLE 1

Five Rationales of Longitudinal Research Outlined by Baltes and Nesselroade (1979)

Rationale	Description
Direct identification of intraindividual change (and stability)	Measuring the same individual (entity) repeatedly allows researchers to identify if and how specific attributes of an individual changed (or remained the same) over time.
Direct identification of interindividual differences (similarity) in intraindividual change	Individuals are likely to differ in the amount of within-person change or in the timing of transitions between developmental stages.
Analysis of interrelationships in behavioral change	Development does not occur in isolation and it is expected that within-person changes in multiple constructs will occur simultaneously and/or sequentially.
Analysis of causes (determinants) of intraindividual change	Within-person change is likely to occur at different rates at different points in time and this rationale is centered on understanding the mechanisms driving the within-person change process.
Analysis of causes (determinants) of interindividual differences in intraindividual change	Since individuals are likely to differ in their amounts or timing of changes, this rationale is focused on understanding the driving forces of these between-person differences in within-person change.

Intraindividual Change. Measuring the same individual (entity) repeatedly allows researchers to identify if and how specific attributes of an individual change (or remain the same) over time. Most often, developmental theories conceptualize and describe within-person change as either incremental or transformational (Ford & Lerner, 1992). The former is observed and identified as a change in the magnitude (quantitative) of the same construct (e.g., mathematics ability) along a continuum over a specific time interval (second through eighth grade). The latter is observed and identified as a change or transition between discrete states (e.g., Piaget's Stage Theory Development; Piaget, 1952). Analytically, the main goal is to obtain a parsimonious and accurate description of how and when attributes of an entity change over time. Importantly, Baltes and Nesselroade noted that stability or constancy over time is a special case of within-person change.

The second rationale for longitudinal research is the *Direct Identification of Interindividual Differences* (*Similarity*) *in Intraindividual Change.* In terms of incremental change, this rationale asks the question—do different individuals change different amounts? For example, do children show different amounts of growth in their mathematics ability from second through eighth grade? In terms of transformation change, the question can be asked in terms of between-person variability in the number of stages passed and between-person variability in the timing of specific transitions. For example, do children vary in the timing of their transition from the preoperational stage to the concrete stage of development? Baltes and Nesselroade suggest that heterogeneity in change is the norm given the "existence of diversity, multidirectionality, and large interindividual differences in developmental outcomes" (p. 24).

The third rationale is the *Analysis of Interrelationships in Behavioral Change* and highlights how development does not occur in isolation. As Baltes and Nesselroade noted, "The examination of interrelationships in change among distinct behavioral classes is particularly important if a structural, holistic approach to development is taken" (p. 25). This holistic approach centers on the idea that the changes in multiple constructs are expected to occur simultaneously and/or sequentially and this rationale encompasses both. Thus, within-person changes in multiple constructs may co-occur because they have similar underlying mechanisms (see McArdle, 1988) or within-person change in one construct may precede within-person change in a second construct (see Grimm, An, McArdle, Zonderman, & Resnick, 2012). For example, changes in mathematics and reading abilities may co-occur (e.g., children who show more positive growth in mathematics tend to show more positive growth in reading) and/or changes in reading may precede or lead to more positive subsequent changes in mathematics (or vice versa). We note that discussing interrelationships among within-person change is challenging because change has both magnitude and direction. Thus, it is necessary to be cautious and avoid eliminating magnitude or direction in such discussions (e.g., *individuals who change more in X change more in Y*—no discussion of direction).

The fourth rationale, *Analysis of Causes (Determinants) of Intraindividual Change*, centers on explaining or accounting for the within-person change process. This rationale highlights that within-person change is likely to occur at different rates at different points in time (e.g., nonlinear change) and is centered on understanding the mechanisms of this change process. Such determinants vary within an individual over time and are therefore dynamic and time-varying.

The fifth and final rationale for longitudinal research is the *Analysis of Causes (Determinants) of Interindividual Differences in Intraindividual Change*. Given that individuals differ in how they change over time, it is logical to assume that measured or unmeasured variables can account for this between-person variability in change. Such variables are often static, time-invariant, and vary between individuals (can be summary information [e.g., mean] of a time-varying variable). Variables or characteristics that may explain between-person differences in within-person change include demographic/background characteristics of the individual, experimental manipulations, additionally measured constructs, and the level of the construct itself. Additionally, Baltes and Nesselroade discuss how determinants of between-person differences in within-person change are not likely to be universal and researchers should expect moderating effects.

INNOVATIONS IN LONGITUDINAL ANALYSIS SINCE 1979

Baltes and Nesselroade's rationales for longitudinal research were presented during a time when researchers were excited about the recent analytical innovations in the field of structural equation modeling (SEM; Jöreskog, 1977). This framework for conducting multivariate analyses was having a significant effect on how researchers thought about, approached, and analyzed data. For the first time it was possible to examine multiple predictors and outcomes, arranged according to theory, within a statistically rigorous framework. Although the possibilities and limitations of this approach were not yet clear, the causal language used in the rationales sought to promote the use of this new and promising framework in developmental research (J. R. Nesselroade, personal communication, July 10, 2013). As substantively and methodologically oriented researchers explored how these and other new methods could be applied to longitudinal data and test developmental theory, the norms for longitudinal analysis were transformed.

The first major developments were prompted by the two-stage (mixed-effects, multilevel) models proposed by Laird and Ware (1982). In this article, two models for longitudinal data were described including, what is now referred to as, the linear growth model and a general repeated measures model. In the linear growth model, within-person change and between-person differences in within-person change could be modeled simultaneously. These two key aspects of the linear growth model mapped directly onto Baltes and Nesselroade's first two rationales for longitudinal research and provided a contrast against Repeated Measures ANOVA (RMANOVA), which assumes that between-person differences in change were nonexistent. Additionally, the model proposed by Laird and Ware (1982) was able to handle incomplete and highly unbalanced data (individuals measured on different time scales; individually varying time metrics), which posited challenges for RMANOVA. Finally, Laird and Ware (1982) discussed how individual characteristics (e.g., sex, race) could be included as a determinant of the between-person variability in within-person change.

In parallel, Meredith and Tisak (1984, 1990) described how the SEM framework could be utilized to study within-person change and between-person differences in change. Extending work by Tucker (1958, 1966), wherein principal component models were applied to the average cross-products matrix obtained from longitudinal data, Meredith and Tisak (1990) described how a restricted common factor model could be used to specify growth models. They explained how the linear growth model could be specified as a confirmatory factor model where the intercept and linear slope were latent variables indicated by the repeated measures variables with a set of fixed factor loadings. Now, the SEM framework could provide information regarding within-person change and between-person differences in within-person change (see Grimm, Castro-Schilo, & Davoudzadeh, 2013). At the time, the SEM framework required complete and balanced data; however, Meredith and Tisak (1984, 1990) discussed how a multiple group model could be used to handle longitudinal data arising from a cohort-sequential design. Additionally, Meredith and Tisak took advantage of several flexibilities provided by the SEM framework. For example, they discussed higher-order polynomial and spline models, described how certain factor loadings for one of the latent variables could be freely estimated (i.e., latent basis, unstructured model) to allow for nonlinear change patterns, fit a negative exponential model, and discussed the flexibility in modeling residual structures and practice effects. Finally, Meredith and Tisak evaluated gender differences in fluid reasoning changes using a multiple group model to examine determinants of the between-person differences in within-person change.

After Meredith and Tisak's (1984, 1990) and Laird and Ware's (1982) work to develop growth models, researchers expanded these foundational methods. For example, McArdle (1986) used the SEM framework to combine growth models with additive genetic models. Using longitudinal twin data, McArdle was able to decompose the variability in the intercept, slope, and unique factors into additive genetic, common environmental, and unique environmental components highlighting how between-person differences in within-person change can have a genetic basis. Additionally, McArdle and Epstein (1987) added, *extension variables* into the growth model, which were time-invariant covariates that had direct effects on the intercept and slope (often referred to as a MIMIC model) to examine determinants of between-person differences in within-person change.

Within the mixed-effect (random coefficient, multilevel) framework, work on the topic was presented by Rogosa and Willett (1985) and Bryk and Raudenbush (1987, 1992). Rogosa and Willett (1985) described various functional models for change (linear, polynomial, exponential, logistic) and then focused their attention on the association between initial status and change in a linear growth model and how this association varies with the location of the intercept. Additionally, they discussed having individual characteristics as predictors of change. Bryk and Raudenbush (1987) described the two-stage modeling approach, model assumptions, estimation of model parameters, reliabilities of initial status and change, and evaluated individual changes in academic performance for a sample of preschool children and the effects of home language and hours of direct classroom instruction on initial status and change. Additionally, Bryk and Raudenbush (1987) highlighted how the study of "individual change has been plagued by inadequacies in conceptualization, measurement, and design" and briefly discussed these inadequacies and potential resolutions. Their 1992 book (Bryk & Raudenbush, 1992) had a chapter dedicated to studying within-person change and the use of time-varying and time-invariant covariates as determinants of within-person change and between-person differences in within-person change.

The *Analysis of Interrelationships in Change* was then studied by McArdle (1988), when he proposed several multivariate extensions of growth models taking advantage of the flexibility available from the SEM framework. One approach was the multivariate growth (parallel process, correlated growth) model where changes in two (or more) variables were jointly examined allowing for the estimation of the correlation between slopes, which is an association among within-person changes. Additional multivariate models proposed by McArdle (1988) included the Factor of Curves Model, whereby associations between intercepts and slopes in multivariate growth models are accounted for by higher-order factors, and the Curve of Factors Model, whereby within-person changes in a latent variable indicated by multiple repeatedly measured variables are modeled (second-order growth model). This model assumes that within-person changes in the multiply repeated variables can be accounted for by a single change trajectory. Within the mixed-effects or multilevel modeling approach, the study of interrelationships in change was presented by MacCallum, Kim, Malarkey, and Kiecolt-Glasser (1997).

The 1990s saw a reemergence on the study of within-person change and between-person differences in within-person change, a realization of the congruence between the SEM and multilevel modeling perspectives for fitting growth models (Willett & Sayer, 1994), and new approaches to studying between-person differences in within-person change (e.g., Muthén & Shedden, 1999). The emergence of improved routines for estimating *nonlinear* mixed-effects models, computing power, and available software enabled researchers to study change patterns where random coefficients entered the model in a nonlinear fashion (see Burchinal & Appelbaum, 1991; Davidian & Giltinan, 1995). Now, developmental processes that followed inherently nonlinear trends could be modeled within the mixed-effects modeling framework allowing researchers to study complex within-person change patterns. In these models, aspects of the nonlinear change function (e.g., individual rate of change at a specific point in time, transitions, asymptotic levels) and between-person differences in these aspects of change were highlighted (see Grimm, Ram, & Hamagami, 2011; Grimm, Zhang, Hamagami, & Mazzocco, 2013; Preacher & Hancock, 2012, 2015). Within the SEM framework, Browne and du Toit (1991) and Browne (1993) showed how nonlinear mixed-effects models could be approximated using Taylor Series expansion, which allowed researchers to continue to take advantage of the flexibility of the SEM framework when modeling inherently nonlinear change processes (see Blozis, 2004; Grimm, Ram, & Estabrook, 2010). In the late 1990s, there was a conceptual shift in how between-person differences in within-person change were studied with the development of the growth mixture (Muthén & Shedden, 1999) and latent class growth models (Nagin, 1999). In growth models, between-person differences in change follow a continuum where between-person differences are solely in magnitude. For example, in the linear growth model, between-person differences in change are contained in the linear slope, a latent variable (random coefficient) assumed to be normally distributed and adequately described by its mean and variance. Thus, in the linear growth model all individuals show linear growth, but are allowed to differ in the amount of linear growth. The latent class growth model allows for differences to emerge as typologies (e.g., linear/quadratic or rapid linear growth/slow linear growth) of change and the growth mixture model allows for between-person differences to manifest as differences in magnitude and typology. That is, it may be the case that all individuals show the same type of growth (e.g., linear) with between-person differences in within-person change following a finite mixture distribution (relaxing the normality assumption in latent growth models). Additionally, between-person differences may be represented by a set (class) of different typologies (see Ram & Grimm, 2009). Importantly, both of these types of between-person differences in within-person change can co-occur (e.g., typological differences between certain individuals and a continuum of differences for individuals who share the same typology). The growth mixture modeling framework also allowed for predictors of class membership (typology) as well as predictors of the between-person differences in within-person change within each class, which expanded the study of determinants of the between-person differences in within-person change. We note that this work must be done cautiously due to its exploratory (data-driven) nature (see Bauer & Curran, 2003; Ram, Grimm, Gatzke-Kopp, & Molenaar, 2011).

In the early 2000s, there was a methodological shift to studying multivariate dynamics as new approaches to studying within-person change were proposed. McArdle and colleagues (McArdle, 2001; McArdle & Hamagami, 2001) discussed the use of latent change (difference) scores for the simultaneous evaluation of within-person change and temporal dynamics with multivariate longitudinal panel data. This framework provided great flexibility for implementing Baltes and Nesselroade's five rationales for longitudinal research (see McArdle & Grimm, 2010; McArdle & Nesselroade, 2014). The latent change score framework combined aspects of growth and time-series models to study within-person change, between-person differences in within-person change, determinants of within-person change, and the determinants of between-person differences in within-person change.

Specifically, as in time-series models, the latent change score framework allows for the possibility of lagged effects from other constructs for modeling determinants for within-person change. Combining the latent change score framework with the finite mixture and multiple group frameworks enabled researchers to study determinants of between-person differences in within-person change as the lagged effects may be dependent on other measured or unmeasured constructs (see Ferrer, Shaywitz, Holahan, Marchione, & Shaywitz, 2010; Grimm, 2006; McArdle & Grimm, 2010).

In addition to all the developments revolving around growth models, there were developments in time-series analyses that were relevant for developmentalists. In studying the determinants of within-person change, dynamic factor models of multivariate time series data were proposed. Engle and Watson (1981) and McArdle (1982) proposed the direct autoregressive factor score model (process factor model) and Geweke and Singleton (1981) and Molenaar (1985) discussed the white-noise (shock) factor model. Both models extended p-technique (Cattell, 1964) factor analysis models to account for time-dependent associations both within and across latent constructs measured over time within an individual.

Additionally, Boker's (2001) research on dynamical systems models led to an increase in the amount of information provided by longitudinal data. Using differential equations models, Boker (2001) modeled associations among acceleration, change, and location at the individual level to yield a damped linear oscillator model, which could model fluctuations in behavior over time. This work was then extended to multivariate time series (e.g., Boker, Neale, & Rausch, 2004) to study determinants of within-person change and interrelationships in within-person change, and to multiperson time series (e.g., Boker, Molenaar, & Nesselroade, 2009) to study between-person differences in within-person change and its determinants.

ADDITIONAL OPPORTUNITIES FOR DEVELOPMENTAL RESEARCHERS

As reviewed above, innovations in statistics and modeling have allowed researchers to examine developmental processes more accurately and precisely. In this section we highlight five additional opportunities that have emerged through the development of new methodologies.

Measurement Invariance

As noted at the outset of the chapter, longitudinal data are obtained when repeated measures are obtained from the same entity in a known sequence. We qualified this statement by indicating that the same variables do not necessarily need to be obtained at each assessment. However, when examining change in a specific construct (e.g., physical height), it is important that the same units of measurement are used (e.g., meters). Typically, the same scales, surveys, questionnaires, and tests are administered and scored in the same way (e.g., total score, average across items) at each occasion. Concurrent with the innovations in modeling within-person change, Meredith, Horn, Reise, Widaman, Millsap and colleagues (Meredith, 1993; Meredith & Horn, 2001; Millsap & Yun-Tein, 2004; Reise, Widaman, & Pugh, 1993; Widaman & Reise, 1997) have elaborated and discussed a variety of approaches to establishing longitudinal measurement invariance in both the factor analytic and item response modeling frameworks to statistically test whether the observed variables measure the same construct in the same scale over time. Notably, these discussions suggest that strong measurement invariance (invariance of factor loadings [discrimination] *and* intercepts [thresholds]) is needed to establish that a given set of scales/tests/surveys/questionnaires assess the same construct in the same metric over time. Only then should we proceed to describe and analyze quantitative change. In following these suggestions, two interesting issues arise.

A failure to find longitudinal measurement invariance suggests either that the structure of the construct measured by the scales/tests/surveys/questionnaires changed over time, or that the scales/tests/surveys/questionnaires were differentially effective at measuring the trait over time. Both are interesting developmental phenomena. In the former case, the longitudinal data provide an opportunity to examine information about change in the structure of between-person differences (in complement to Baltes & Nesselroade's focus on between-person differences in change; see also Nesselroade, 1991). In the latter case, tracking of the specific characteristic over time requires that the scales/tests/surveys/questionnaires are adapted or adjusted over time (i.e., kept age appropriate). Application of test-linking methods has expanded the possibilities for maintaining valid measurement through larger and larger windows of development (e.g., Edwards & Wirth, 2009; McArdle, Grimm, Hamagami, Bowles, & Meredith, 2009) while targeting assessments to each individual.

Between-Person Differences in Timing

As noted above, the study of between-person differences in within-person change has been greatly facilitated through the use of growth models. Model parameters typically provide a description of the average trajectory and the magnitude of deviations around the average trajectory. Interpretations of the model's parameters tend to highlight between-person differences in relation to the construct of interest (the y-axis). For example, as shown in Figure 1, researchers are often interested in between-person differences in the level of Y at a specific point in time (e.g., time $= t_3$). However, as noted in the

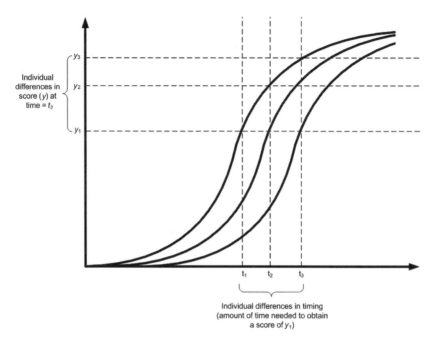

FIGURE 1.—Illustration of how changes in level (*y*-axis) can be due to changes in timing (*x*-axis).

descriptions of development (e.g., Ford & Lerner, 1992; Thelen & Smith, 1996), two key aspects of within-person change are the *timing* and *duration of change*. While these aspects of change are often examined using event history analysis, it may also be useful to consider how they manifest within the growth modeling framework. The differences in the trajectories shown in Figure 1 are actually due to differences in the *timing* of growth (i.e., variance along the *x*-axis). That is, all three individuals show the same change function (same initial and ultimate value, amount of growth, and rate of growth), but are offset in time. Thus, differences in level or rate of change at any given point in time are actually due to differences in timing. Through transformations or inclusion of additional parameters, growth models can often be parameterized in ways that facilitate the testing of developmental hypotheses regarding timing and duration of change (see Cudeck & du Toit, 2002). One approach to studying individual differences in timing is through the use of multiphase models where both the between-person differences in the rate of change within each phase and in the between-person differences in timing and duration of each developmental period can be studied (Cudeck & Klebe, 2002; Wang & McArdle, 2008).

Conceptually, the implication is that we should consider within-person change in two complementary ways. Usually, we quantify change with respect to the magnitude of change a person displays over specific span of time (e.g., rate of change per year; Δy with Δt held constant). In complement we might also consider how much time it takes for a person to change a specific amount (Δt with Δy held constant). Substantively, we are sometimes interested in the former and, at times, we are interested in the latter. Both approaches are available and should be incorporated—precisely mapping model parameters to the specific conceptualization that follows best from the theory of change (see also Preacher & Hancock, 2015).

Dynamics of Within-Person Change

The move toward difference and differential models has expanded the vocabulary of models that are used to describe within-person change processes. The use of first differences and first derivatives (dy/dt) represent the velocity/rate of change of the process under study. Extension to second differences and second derivatives (d^2y/dt^2) represent how quickly the rate of change of the process under study is changing and highlight how the rate of change is rarely constant. In particular, work by Boker, DeBoeck, and colleagues (Boker, 2001; DeBoeck & Bergman, 2013) highlights the possibilities for using differential equation based models to examine between-person differences, predictors, and correlates of acceleration. In complement, research by Hamagami and McArdle (2007) illustrate how difference equations can be used to capture time-dependent associations among within-person states, changes, and accelerations. Additionally, Grimm et al. (2013) recently showed how the latent change score and latent acceleration frameworks could be utilized to study between-person differences in and determinants of within-person change and acceleration. These models provide opportunities to more precisely capture the inherent dynamics of individual development.

Stochastic Aspects of Intraindividual Change

In the dialectic surrounding longitudinal study of lifespan development, Nesselroade (1991) made a distinction between within-person change—changes that proceed slowly and are relatively enduring, and within-person variability—changes that proceed more quickly and are relatively reversible. The former are typically characterized as directional change or development and evaluated using growth models and related methods. The latter are typically characterized as fluctuations, cycles, or noise and modeled using time series methods (Ram & Gerstorf,

2009). Following this distinction researchers have applied the rationales for longitudinal research to the study of within-person variability (e.g., investigating the determinants of within-person variability and between-person differences therein). Generally, the extent of within-person variability in any process differs substantially across persons and is uniquely related to a variety of important constructs and life events. For example, Nesselroade and Salthouse (2004) found that, among a sample of 20–91 year olds, the average amount of within-person variability in perceptual-motor performance over a 2-week interval was approximately half the magnitude of between-person variability. Across multiple studies and domains, between-person differences in within-person variability were related to age, performance, impending death, neuropsychological disorders, and other characteristics (e.g., MacDonald, Nyberg, & Bäckman, 2006; Ram, Gerstorf, Lindenberger, & Smith, 2011; Salthouse, 2007). In describing within-person variability, its determinants and how it differs across persons, researchers are making use of a variety of longitudinal time-series models, including discrete time state-space, latent Markov, and stochastic differential equation models (see Ram & Gerstorf, 2009), and extensions of mixed-effects models (see Hedeker, Mermelstein, & Demirtas, 2008). A key conceptual shift that is pushing this work forward is the idea that within-person variability is a key mechanism of change. For example, in the state-space framework, random shocks prompt within-person change and stabilization (see Browne & Nesselroade, 2005). Rather than viewing change as the product of a deterministic function, models of within-person variability often seek to model how the individual will respond to endogenous and exogenous influences that have not yet occurred. Consistent with the progression in other fields, these models are opening up new conversations about how process-oriented models can support prediction and optimization of individual development (Molenaar & Lo, 2012; Ram, Brose, & Molenaar, 2013; Zhou et al., 2010).

Change, Acceleration, and Variability as Determinants (Causes)

Baltes and Nesselroade's (1979) rationales maintain a focus on within-person change as the primary outcome of interest. A next step is to understand how those changes connect to individuals' futures. That is, we need to model how within-person change, acceleration, and/or variability during an earlier phase of development affects and influences risk of subsequent (distal) outcomes. For example, Grimm et al. (2012) studied how recent changes in lateral ventricle size were predictive of subsequent declines in memory performance for a sample of older adults. An additional example from studying within-person change can be found in the work of Kovatchev and colleagues (Kovatchev et al., 1999,

2000), where the rate of change in blood glucose was found to be predictive of subsequent severe hypoglycemia in a sample of type I diabetics.

Time-Dependent Effects, Nonstationarity, and Multiple Time Scales

The processes driving within-person change, acceleration, and variability are influenced by a variety of internal and external factors, which evolve over time and differ across contexts (Ford & Lerner, 1992). From a modeling perspective, this suggests a need to consider if and how our descriptions of change and its associations with other variables differ with age, cohort, and time (Schaie, 1986). For example, Dogan, Stockdale, Widaman, and Conger (2010) found that the time-lagged association between alcohol use and the number of sexual partners was dependent upon age, such that the strength of the association diminished as participants progressed from late adolescence through early adulthood. In a similar vein, Kim and Nelson (1999) outlined the use and estimation of multiregime state space models (see also Hamaker, Grasman, & Kamphuis, 2010) where the core idea is that the ongoing processes may switch among two or more regimes. That is, for one period of time, the process may be well described by one set of parameters (regime 1). However, after some event, change in context, or on particular occasions, the process is described by a different set of parameters (regime 2). Models such as these that accommodate nonstationarity (processes whose dynamics change over time) are needed to articulate how human behavior is co-constructed (Baltes, Reuter-Lorenz, & Rösler, 2006; Li, 2003) by processes occurring at many levels and across multiple time scales.

On that note, we highlight how multiple time scale approaches are emerging in a variety of fields. For example, dynamic factor analysis models have been extended to include time-varying parameters (Chow, Hamaker, Fujita, & Boker, 2009; Molenaar & Ram, 2010) and used to describe changes in the manner in which partners interact with one another (Molenaar, Sinclair, Rovine, Ram, & Corneal, 2009). Although computationally challenging (and necessarily data intensive) numerical methods are being developed to address multiscale problems, including multigrid methods, domain decomposition methods, fast multiple methods, adaptive mesh refinement techniques, and multiresolution methods using wavelets (Weinan & Enquist, 2003). As more data become available (e.g., using diary- and experience sampling-based multiple burst designs; Ram, Coccia, et al., 2013), such methods will become increasingly useful in identifying and modeling the layered complexity of time- and context-dependent differences in within-person change. For example, many theories of development consider individuals as systems capable of both self-regulation, wherein coordinated action of subsystems compensate for changing conditions in the environment and maintain homeostasis, and adaptive self-organization, wherein the system as a whole transforms to accommodate change in or to challenge the existing configuration (e.g., Ford & Lerner, 1992; Thelen & Smith, 1996). For example, modeling how self-regulatory systems responding to "micro-challenges" encountered in daily life reorganize and adapt in response to "macro-challenges" and major life shifts may provide additional insights for both normative development (e.g., reorganizations occurring during puberty) and nonnormative development (e.g., reorganizations invoked by major life events; see e.g., Ram et al., 2013 for empirical example).

FINAL THOUGHTS

The progression of developmental inquiry has sometimes been characterized as a dance between theory and method—where, at times, theoretical considerations lead to methodological innovations, and, at other times, methodological advances lead to elaboration and refinement of theory. Back in 1979 Baltes and Nesselroade elaborated five rationales for longitudinal research and in the four decades since, researchers have developed and applied new tools capable of articulating those rationales. At the same time, these innovations have prompted consideration of a new set of issues, five of which we have been described here.

In recent years, a new partner has joined this dance. Recent advances in mobile and computing technology have opened new possibilities to obtain intensive longitudinal data. The electronic devices many of us now carry as we go about our daily lives provide a wide array of opportunities to collect more data from more participants. The availability of such data has tremendous implications for the study of within-person change, acceleration, and variability—from both the theoretical and methodological points of view. In particular, the density of data being collected will likely accelerate the conceptualization and use of time as a continuous (rather than discrete) variable (see Oud & Folmer, 2011; Oud & Jansen, 2000; Steele & Ferrer, 2011) and the use of coupled differential equations to describe the time-dependent relations among multiple characteristics across multiple time scales (e.g., Ram et al., 2013). Shifting to this vernacular will give immediate access to the many models that are being used in other fields to study change processes.

The movement to intense data streams will lead to several methodological issues that will require deep thought. Currently, the majority of methods and models utilized in longitudinal researcher focus on a theoretical model and we examine how well the model accounts for the associations in our data. We see this as a static research process, as opposed to a dynamic research process where we are continually building on new data to fine tune our models. We also expect a shift toward prediction, such that longitudinal researchers will focus on predicting future states, particularly at the individual level. With this goal in mind, researchers must consider optimal ways to create such prediction models, potentially building on exploratory data analysis models, propose new methods for internal and external cross-validation of these prediction models, and balance the need for individual prediction models while attempting to find nomothetic laws.

REFERENCES

Baltes, P. B., & Nesselroade, J. R. (1979). History and rationale of longitudinal research. In J. R. Nesselroade & P. B. Baltes (Eds.), *Longitudinal research in the study of behavior and development* (pp. 1–39). New York, NY: Academic Press.

Baltes, P. B., Reuter-Lorenz, P. A., & Rösler, F. (Eds.) (2006). *Lifespan development and the brain: The perspective of biocultural co-constructivism.* New York, NY: Cambridge University Press.

Bauer, D. J. & Curran, P. J. (2003). Distributional assumptions of growth mixture models: Implications for over-extraction of latent trajectory classes. *Psychological Methods*, 8, 338–363.

Blozis, S. A. (2004). Structured latent curve models for the study of change in multivariate repeated measures. *Psychological Methods*, 9, 334–353.

Boker, S. M. (2001). Differential structural equation modeling of intraindividual variability. In L. M. Collins & A. G. Sayer (Eds.), *New methods for the analysis of change* (pp. 5–27). Washington, DC: American Psychological Association.

Boker, S. M., Molenaar, P. C. M., & Nesselroade, J. R. (2009). Issues in intraindividual variability: Individual differences in equilibria and dynamics over multiple time scales. *Psychology and Aging*, **24**, 858–862.

Boker, S. M., Neale, M. C., & Rausch, J. R. (2004). Latent differential equation modeling with multivariate multi-occasion indicators. In K. van Montfort, J. Oud, & A. Satorra (Eds), *Recent developments on structural equation models* (pp. 151–174). Dordrecht, Netherlands: Kluwer Academic Publishers.

Bowles, R. (2006). *Item response models for intratask change to examine the impacts of proactive interference on the aging of working memory span.* Unpublished Doctoral Dissertation, University of Virginia.

Browne, M. W. (1993). Structured latent curve models. In C. M. Cuadras & C. R. Rao (Eds.), *Multivariate analysis: Future directions 2* (pp. 171–197). Amsterdam: Elsevier Science.

Browne, M. W., & du Toit, S. C. H. (1991). Models for learning data. In L. Collins & J. L. Horn (Eds.), *Best methods for the analysis of change* (pp. 47–68). Washington, DC: American Psychological Association.

Browne, M. W., & Nesselroade, J. R. (2005). Representing psychological processes with dynamic factor models: Some promising uses and extensions of ARMA time series models. In A. Maydeu-Olivares & J. J. McArdle (Eds.), *Psychometrics: A festschrift to Roderick P. McDonald* (pp. 415–452). Mahwah, NJ: Erlbaum.

Bryk, A. S., & Raudenbush, S. W. (1987). Application of hierarchical linear models to assess change. *Psychological Bulletin*, **101**, 147–158.

Bryk, A. S., & Raudenbush, S. W. (1992). *Hierarchical linear models in social and behavioral research: Applications and data analysis methods* (1st ed.). Newbury Park, CA: Sage Publications.

Burchinal, M., & Appelbaum, M. I. (1991). Estimating individual developmental functions: Methods and their assumptions. *Child Development*, **62**, 23–43.

Cattell, R. B. (1964). Validity and reliability: A proposed more basic set of concepts. *Journal of Educational Psychology*, **55**, 1–22.

Chow, S.-M., Hamaker, E. L., Fujita, F., & Boker, S. M. (2009). Representing time-varying cyclic dynamics using multiple subject state-space models. *British Journal of Mathematical and Statistical Psychology*, **62**, 683–716.

Cudeck, R., & du Toit, S. H. C. (2002). A version of quadratic regression with interpretable parameters. *Multivariate Behavioral Research*, **37**, 501–519.

Cudeck R., & Klebe, K. J. (2002). Multiphase mixed-effects models for repeated measures data. *Psychological Methods*, **7**, 41–63.

Davidian, M., & Giltinan, D. M. (1995). *Nonlinear models for repeated measures data*. New York, NY: Chapman and Hall.

Dearborn, W. F., & Rothney, J. W. M. (1941). *Predicting the child's development*. Cambridge, MA: Sci-Art Publishers.

DeBoeck, P., & Bergman, C. S. (2013). The reservoir model: A differential equation model of psychological regulation. *Psychological Methods*, **18**, 237–256.

Dogan, S. J., Stockdale, G. D., Widaman, K. F., & Conger, R. D. (2010). Developmental relations and patterns of change between alcohol use and number of sexual partners from adolescence through adulthood. *Developmental Psychology*, **46**, 1747–1759.

Edwards, M. C., & Wirth, R. J. (2009). Measurement and study of change. *Research in Human Development*, **6**, 74–96.

Engle, R., & Watson, M. (1981). A one-factor multivariate time series model of metropolitan wage rates. *Journal of the American Statistical Association*, **76**, 774–481.

Ferrer, E., Shaywitz, B. A., Holahan, J. M, Marchione, K., & Shaywitz, S. E. (2010). Uncoupling of reading and IQ over time: Empirical evidence for a definition of dyslexia. *Psychological Science*, **21**, 93–101.

Ford, D. H., & Lerner, R. M. (1992). *Developmental systems theory: An integrative approach*. Thousand Oaks, CA: Sage Publications.

Gerstorf, D., & Ram, N. (2013). Inquiry into terminal decline: Five objectives for future study. *The Gerontologist*, **53**, 727–737.

Geweke, J. F., & Singleton, K. J. (1981). Maximum likelihood "confirmatory" factor analysis of economic time series. *International Economic Review*, **22**, 37–54.

Grimm, K. J. (2006). *A longitudinal dynamic analysis of the impacts of reading on mathematical ability in children and adolescents*. Unpublished Doctoral Dissertation, University of Virginia.

Grimm, K. J., An, Y., McArdle, J. J., Zonderman, A. B., & Resnick, S. M. (2012). Recent changes leading to subsequent changes: Extensions of multivariate latent difference score models. *Structural Equation Modeling: A Multidisciplinary Journal*, **19**, 268–292.

Grimm, K. J., Castro-Schilo, L., & Davoudzadeh, P. (2013). Modeling interindividual change in nonlinear growth models with latent change scores. *GeroPsych*, **26**, 153–162.

Grimm, K. J., Ram, N., & Estabrook, R. (2010). Nonlinear structured growth mixture models in Mplus and OpenMx. *Multivariate Behavioral Research*, **45**, 887–909.

Grimm, K. J., Ram, N., & Hamagami, F. (2011). Nonlinear growth curves in developmental research. *Child Development*, **82**, 1357–1372.

Grimm, K. J., Zhang, Z., Hamagami, F., & Mazzocco, M. (2013). Modeling nonlinear change via latent change and latent acceleration frameworks: Examining velocity and acceleration of growth trajectories. *Multivariate Behavioral Research*, **48**, 117–143.

Hamagami, F., & McArdle, J. J. (2007). Dynamic extensions of latent difference score models. In S. M. Boker & M. J. Wenger (Eds.), *Data analytic techniques for dynamical systems* (pp. 47–86). New Jersey: Erlbaum.

Hamaker, E. L., Grasman, R. P. P., & Kamphuis, J. H. (2010). Regime-switching models to study psychological processes. In: P. M. C. Molenaar & K. Newell (Eds.), *Individual pathways of change: Statistical models for analyzing learning and development* (pp. 155–168). Washington, DC: American Psychological Association.

Hedeker, D., Mermelstein, R. J., & Demirtas, H. (2008). An application of a mixed-effects location scale model for analysis of Ecological Momentary Assessment (EMA) data. *Biometrics*, **64**, 627–634.

Jöreskog, K. G. (1977). Structural equation models in the social sciences: Specification estimation, and testing. In P. R. Krishnaiah (Ed.), *Applications of statistics* (pp. 265–287). Amsterdam: North-Holland.

Kim, C. J., & Nelson, C. R. (1999). *State-space models with regime switching: Classical and Gibbs-sampling approaches with applications.* Cambridge, MA: MIT Press.

Kovatchev, B. P., Cox, D. J., Farhy, L. S., Straume, M., Gonder-Frederick, L., & Clarke, W. L. (2000). Episodes of severe hypoglycemia in type 1 diabetes are preceded and followed within 48 hours by measurable disturbances in blood glucose. *The Journal of Clinical Endocrinology & Metabolism*, **85**, 4287–4292.

Kovatchev, B. P., Farhy, L. S., Cox, D. J., Straume, M., Yankov, V. I., Gonder-Frederick, L. A., et al. (1999). Modeling insulin-glucose dynamics during insulin induced hypoglycemia. Evaluation of glucose counterregulation. *Journal of Theoretical Medicine*, **1**, 313–323.

Laird, N. M., & Ware, J. H. (1982). Random-effects models for longitudinal data. *Biometrics*, **38**, 963–974.

Li, S.-C. (2003). Biocultural orchestration of developmental plasticity across levels: The interplay of biology and culture in shaping the mind and behavior across the lifespan. *Psychological Bulletin*, **129**, 171–194.

MacCallum, R. C., Kim, C., Malarkey, W. B., & Kielcolt-Glaser, J. K. (1997). Studying multivariate change using multilevel models and latent curve models. *Multivariate Behavioral Research*, **32**, 215–253.

MacDonald, S. W. S., Nyberg, L., & Bäckman, L. (2006). Intra-individual variability in behavior: Links to brain structure, neurotransmission and neuronal activity. *Trends in Neurosciences*, **29**, 474–480.

McArdle, J. J. (1982). *Structural equation modeling of an individual system: Preliminary results from "a case study in episodic alcoholism."* Unpublished manuscript, Department of Psychology, University of Denver.

McArdle, J. J. (1986). Latent variable growth within behavior genetic models. *Behavior Genetics*, **16**, 163–200.

McArdle, J. J. (1988). Dynamic but structural modeling of repeated measures data. In J. R. Nesselroade & R. B. Cattell (Eds.), *The handbook of multivariate psychology* (2nd ed., pp. 561–614). New York, NY: Plenum Press.

McArdle, J. J. (2001). A latent difference score approach to longitudinal dynamic structural analysis. In R. Cudeck, S. du Toit, & D. Sörbom (Eds.), *Structural equation modeling: Present and future. A Festschrift in honor of Karl Jöreskog* (pp. 341–380). Lincolnwood, IL: Scientific Software International.

McArdle, J. J., & Epstein, D. (1987). Latent growth curves within developmental structural equation models. *Child Development*, **58**, 110–133.

McArdle, J. J., & Grimm, K. J. (2010). Five steps in latent curve and latent change score modeling with longitudinal data. In K. van Montfort, J. Oud, & A. Satorra (Eds), *Longitudinal research with latent variables* (pp. 245–273). Verlag Berlin Heidelberg: Springer.

McArdle, J. J., Grimm, K. J., Hamagami, F., Bowles, R., & Meredith, W. (2009). Modeling life-span growth curves of cognition using longitudinal data with multiple samples and changing scales of measurement. *Psychological Methods*, **14**, 126–149.

McArdle, J. J., & Hamagami, F. (2001). Latent difference score structural models for linear dynamic analyses with incomplete longitudinal data. In L. M. Collins & A. G. Sayer (Eds.), *New methods for the analysis of change* (pp. 137–176). Washington, DC: American Psychological Association.

McArdle, J. J. & Nesselroade, J. R. (2014). *Longitudinal data analysis using structural equation models*. Washington, DC: American Psychological Association.

Meredith, W. (1993). Measurement invariance, factor analysis and factor invariance. *Psychometrika*, **58**, 525–544.

Meredith, W., & Horn, J. L. (2001). The role of factorial invariance in modeling growth and change. In L. M. Collins & A. G. Sayer (Eds.), *New methods for the analysis of change* (pp. 203–240). Washington, DC: American Psychological Association.

Meredith, W., & Tisak, J. (1984). *"Tuckerizing" curves*. Paper presented at the annual meeting of the Psychometric Society, Santa Barbara, CA.

Meredith, W., & Tisak, J. (1990). Latent curve analysis. *Psychometrika*, **55**, 107–122.

Millsap, R. E., & Yun-Tein, J. (2004). Assessing factorial invariance in ordered-categorical measures. *Multivariate Behavioral Research*, **39**, 479–515.

Molenaar, P. C. M. (1985). A dynamic factor model for the analysis of multivariate time series. *Psychometrika*, **50**, 181–202.

Molenaar, P. C. M., & Lo, L. (2012). Dynamic factor analysis and control of developmental processes. In: B. Laursen, T. D. Little, & N.A. Card (Eds.), *Handbook of developmental research methods* (pp. 333–349). New York, NY: Guilford Press.

Molenaar, P. C. M., & Ram, N. (2010). Dynamic modeling and optimal control of intraindividual variation: A computation paradigm for nonergodic psychological processes. In P. C. M. Molenaar & N. Ram, *Statistical methods for modeling human dynamics: An interdisciplinary dialogue* (pp. 13–37). New York, NY: Routledge/Taylor & Francis Group.

Molenaar, P. C. M., Sinclair, K. O., Rovine, M. J., Ram, N., & Corneal, S. E. (2009). Analyzing developmental processes on an individual level using nonstationary time series modeling. *Developmental Psychology*, **45**, 260–271.

Muthén, B., & Shedden, K. (1999). Finite mixture modeling with mixture outcomes using the EM algorithm. *Biometrics*, **55**, 463–469.

Nagin, D. S. (1999). Analyzing developmental trajectories: A semi-parametric, group-based approach. *Psychological Methods, 4*, 139–177.

Nesselroade, J. R. (1991). Interindividual differences in intraindividual change. In L. Collins & J. L. Horn (Eds.), *Best methods for the analysis of change* (pp. 92–105). Washington, DC: American Psychological Association.

Nesselroade, J. R., & Salthouse, T. A. (2004). Methodological and theoretical implications of intraindividual variability in perceptual-motor performance. *Journal of Gerontology, 59B*, 49–55.

Oud, J. H. L. & Folmer, H. (2011). Reply to Steele & Ferrer: Modeling oscillation, approximately or exactly? *Multivariate Behavioral Research, 46*, 985–993.

Oud, J. H. L., & Jansen, R. A. R. G. (2000). Continuous time state space modeling of panel data by means of SEM. *Psychometrika, 65*, 199–215.

Piaget, J. (1952). *The origins of intelligence in children*. New York, NY: International University Press.

Preacher, K. J., & Hancock, G. R. (2012). On interpretable reparameterizations of linear and nonlinear latent growth curve models. In J. R. Harring & G. R. Hancock (Eds.), *Advances in longitudinal methods in the social and behavioral sciences* (pp. 25–58). Charlotte, NC: Information Age Publishing.

Preacher, K. J., & Hancock, G. R. (2015). Meaningful aspects of change as novel random coefficients: A general method for reparameterizing longitudinal models. *Psychological Methods, 20*, 84–101.

Ram, N., Brose, A., & Molenaar, P. C. M. (2013). Dynamic factor analysis: Modeling person-specific process. In N. Ram, A. Brose, & P. C. M. Molenaar (Eds.), *The Oxford handbook of quantitative methods (Vol 2): Statistical analysis* (pp. 441–457). New York, NY: Oxford University Press.

Ram, N., Coccia, M., Conroy, D., Lorek, A., Orland, B., Pincus, A., et al. (2013). Behavioral landscapes and change in behavioral landscapes: A multiple time-scale density distribution approach. *Research in Human Development, 10*, 88–110.

Ram, N., & Gerstorf, D. (2009). Time-structured and net intraindividual variability: Tools for examining the development of dynamic characteristics and processes. *Psychology and Aging, 24*, 778–791.

Ram, N., Gerstorf, D., Lindenberger, U., & Smith, J. (2011). Developmental change and intraindividual variability: Relating cognitive aging to cognitive plasticity, cardiovascular lability, and emotional diversity. *Psychology and Aging, 26*, 363–371.

Ram, N., & Grimm, K. J. (2009). Growth mixture modeling: A method for identifying differences in longitudinal change among unobserved groups. *International Journal of Behavioral Development, 33*, 565–576.

Ram, N., Grimm, K., Gatzke-Kopp, L., & Molenaar, P. C. M. (2011). Longitudinal mixture models and the identification of archetypes: Action-adventure, mystery, science fiction, fantasy, or romance? In B. Laursen, T. Little, & N. Card (Eds.), *Handbook of developmental research methods* (pp. 481–500). New York, NY: Guilford.

Reise, S. P., Widaman, K. F., & Pugh, R. H. (1993). Confirmatory factor analysis and item response theory: Two approaches for exploring measurement invariance. *Psychological Bulletin, 114*, 552–566.

Rogosa, D. R., & Willett, J. B. (1985). Understanding correlates of change by modeling individual differences in growth. *Psychometrika, 50*, 203–228.

Salthouse, T. A. (2007). Implications of within-person variability in cognitive and neuropsychological functioning for the interpretation of change. *Neuropsychology*, **21**(4), 401–411.

Schaie, K. W. (1986). Beyond calendar definitions of age, time and cohort: The general developmental model revisited. *Developmental Review*, **6**, 252–277.

Steele, J., & Ferrer, E. (2011). Latent differential equation modeling of self-regulatory and coregulatory affective processes. *Multivariate Behavioral Research*, **46**, 956–984.

Thelen, E., & Smith, L. B. (1996). *A dynamic systems approach to the development of cognition and action*. Cambridge, Massachusetts: MIT press.

Tucker, L. R. (1958). Determination of parameters of a functional relation by factor analysis. *Psychometrika*, **23**, 19–23.

Tucker, L. R. (1966). Some mathematical notes on three-mode factor analysis. *Psychometrika*, **21**, 279–311.

Wang, L., & McArdle, J. J. (2008). A simulation study comparison of Bayesian estimation with conventional methods for estimating unknown change points. *Structural Equation Modeling*, **15**, 52–74.

Weinan, E., & Enquist, B. (2003). The heterogeneous multiscale methods. *Communications in Mathematical Sciences*, **1**, 87–132.

Widaman, K. F., & Reise, S. P. (1997). Exploring the measurement invariance of psychological instruments: Applications in the substance use domain. In K. J. Bryant, M. Windle, & S. G. West (Eds.), *The science of prevention: Methodological advances from alcohol and substance use research* (pp. 281–324). Washington, DC: American Psychological Association.

Willett, J. B., & Sayer, A. G. (1994). Using covariance structure analysis to detect correlates and predictors of change over time. *Psychological Bulletin*, **116**, 363–381.

Zhou, J., Wang, Q., Molenaar, P. C. M., Ulbrecht, J., Gold, C., & Rovine, M. (2010). Receding horizon control of type 1 diabetes based on data-driven linear time-varying state-space model. *Proceedings of American Control Conference*, Baltimore, MD, 2033–2038.

V. DESIGN-BASED APPROACHES FOR IMPROVING MEASUREMENT IN DEVELOPMENTAL SCIENCE

Jonathan Rush and Scott M. Hofer

This article is part of the issue "Developmental Methodology" Card (Issue Author). For a full listing of articles in this issue, see: http://onlinelibrary.wiley.com/doi/10.1111/mono.v82.2/issuetoc.

The study of change and variation within individuals, and the relative comparison of changes across individuals, relies on the assumption that observed measurements reflect true change in the construct being measured. Measurement properties that change over time, contexts, or people pose a fundamental threat to validity and lead to ambiguous conclusions about change and variation. We highlight such measurement issues from a within-person perspective and discuss the merits of measurement-intensive research designs for improving precision of both within-person and between-person analysis. In general, intensive measurement designs, potentially embedded within long-term longitudinal studies, provide developmental researchers an opportunity to more optimally capture within-person change and variation as well as provide a basis to understand changes in dynamic processes and determinants of these changes over time.

The study of change and variation within individuals, and the relative comparison of changes across individuals, relies on the assumption that observed measurements reflect true change in the construct being measured. Measurement properties that change over time within a person, across

Corresponding author: Jonathan Rush, Department of Psychology, University of Victoria, Victoria, BC V8W 2Y2; email: jrush@uvic.ca

Research reported in this publication was supported by National Institute on Aging of the National Institutes of Health under grant number P01AG043362 and R01AG050720. The content is solely the responsibility of the authors and does not necessarily represent the official views of the National Institutes of Health.

DOI: 10.1111/mono.12299

contexts, or individuals pose a fundamental threat to the validity of a study and ambiguate conclusions about change and variation. That observed measurements are a reflection of true scores is critical to the study of individual differences and in understanding change and variation within individuals over time.

A variety of research designs, including decisions about the number, frequency, and types of measurements, are used to understand developmental and aging-related processes. Various statistical models can be applied to answer specific questions regarding population average patterns of change, individual differences in level and rate of change, and multivariate dynamics of within-person variation. Each observed score carries many sources of variation that influence our models. Design features play an important role in the ability to disentangle the different sources of variation. Figure 1 shows how an individual's observed scores over time can be broken down into a representation of population average level and slope, individual deviation from level and slope, and systematic within-person deviations from the individual slope as distinct from random error. Perhaps the most important feature of longitudinal studies is the opportunity to distinguish between-person age differences from within-person age variation and change and how individuals differ in terms of within-person age change. Notably, measurement error is often confounded with reliable within-person variation in cross-sectional and typical longitudinal designs, with such variation within and across days often the focus of intensive measurement (e.g., daily diary) designs.

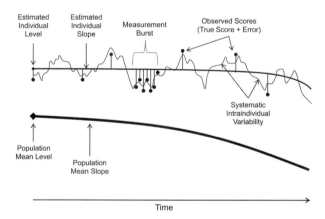

FIGURE 1.—Theoretical decomposition of an individual's observed scores into population mean level and slope, individual deviation from level and slope, and systematic intraindividual deviations from the individual slope as distinct from measurement error.

68

Important longitudinal design features (e.g., Lerner, Schwartz, & Phelps, 2009) include whether the sample at baseline is age-heterogeneous or homogeneous (which may complicate interpretation given confounds with birth cohort and mortality selection), and the number and spacing of measurement occasions as this will affect the types of within-person models of change that can be reliably estimated (see Rast & Hofer, 2014). Design features can be combined in a number of ways to answer research questions that vary in scope from population change across birth cohorts to daily dynamics of within-person processes. Fundamental to developmental research is measurement with the question of how best to measure processes that vary and change within person?

Change in physiological, cognitive, and social functioning early in the lifespan can be relatively rapid. Measurement in different developmental periods often require the use of different measures, with different emphases given changing contexts related to home, school, work, and retirement. Kagan (1980) described the need for identifying a construct using different measures, referred to as phenotypic discontinuity, with the construct retaining its meaning across developmental periods (i.e., heterotypic continuity). There have been a number of recent advances and applications for bridging measurements across developmental periods to maintain continuity in the construct, permitting the analysis of individual change (e.g., McArdle, Grimm, Hamagami, Bowles, & Meredith, 2009).

In this chapter, we expand on these previous developments with an emphasis on measurement issues from a within-person perspective, and highlight benefits for measurement and understanding developmental dynamics from measurement-intensive research designs (e.g., Hoffman, 2007; Nesselroade, 1991; Rast, MacDonald, & Hofer, 2012; Salthouse & Nesselroade, 2010; Walls, Barta, Stawski, Collyer, & Hofer, 2012). Such designs better enable developmental researchers the opportunity to capture within-person change and variation as well as provide potentially better foundations to understand stability and change dynamics in developmental processes. While we highlight the importance of considering design features for improving measurements in this article, we want to also point to the value of evaluating factorial invariance of measurements and subsequent measurement development for repeated measurement designs (e.g., Bontempo, Grouzet, & Hofer, 2012; Bontempo & Hofer, 2007; Ferrer, Balluerka, & Widaman, 2008; Meredith & Horn, 2001).

SAMPLING TIME: ISSUES FOR THE MEASUREMENT OF CHANGE AND VARIATION

The majority of measurement development has been in terms of between-person differences, where the level of a construct is captured relative to other individuals. These between-person differences are predominantly captured at a single occasion in time. Conclusions about individual differences and long-term change are dependent upon accurately measuring an individual's characteristic level at a specific time period. Both widely spaced longitudinal designs and single occasion, cross-sectional, designs are susceptible to biases (e.g., recall error) that threaten the accurate measurement of true level during a given period of time. This subsequently obscures the accuracy of the measurement of long-term change and between-person differences.

Issues With Single Occasion Measurements

Cross-sectional and widely spaced longitudinal measures fail to account for the potential variability around trait levels. When measures vary both within-person across time as well as between people, measuring only once forces all systematic within-person variations to be grouped together and treated as random measurement error. As a result, the cross-sectional measure carries both between-person information (i.e., characteristic individual level) and within-person information (i.e., deviations from individual level) with no possibility of disentangling the two sources of variation with only a single measurement (e.g., Curran & Bauer, 2011; Hoffman & Stawski, 2009). For example, an individual could be higher than others on a measure of well-being because they are a generally a happier person, or their well-being level could be affected by them having a particularly good day, which elevates their score higher than their typical level (Schwarz & Strack, 1999). Assuming that a construct is stable can be problematic when the construct does indeed systematically vary over time and can lead to conclusions about individual differences that are confounded with within-person variance (e.g., Rush & Hofer, 2014).

Many constructs in developmental research are captured via recall of behaviors, attitudes, or experiences within a delimited period of time (e.g., well-being, victimization, substance use). These measures typically rely on self-report recall, or the recall of other informants (e.g., friends, family, teachers; Allen, Chango, Szwedo, Schad, & Marston, 2012; Jordan & Graham, 2012; Ladd & Kochenderfer-Ladd, 2002). The retrospective time-range of cross-sectional measures can vary widely from the previous months or years, to asking about global levels. When measures are derived solely from a single occasion, there are a number of biases that distort the true level of the construct. Global measures are susceptible to retrospection bias, particularly when the assessment period is farther removed from the period of recall (Schwarz, Kahneman, & Xu, 2009). A potentially more problematic issue with global measures are social desirability biases, which include (1) impression management, where individuals purpose-fully attempt to present themselves more favorably and (2) deceptive self-enhancement, where individuals unintentionally respond according to their self-image, rather than actual behaviors/experiences (Barta, Tennen, & Litt, 2012).

An inability to accurately recall the events of the distant past (e.g., months/year) often results in the responses being based on a top-down approach of relying on a global self-perception of themselves and how someone who fits that self-perception would act (Schwarz, 2012). For example, parents who rated the enjoyment they experience while spending time with their children via a global self-report consistently rank it as among the most enjoyable things they do (Juster, 1985). However, when rating their enjoyment with their children on a particular day, through an end-of-day reconstruction, they rated it as among the least enjoyable events of the day (Kahneman, Krueger, Schkade, Schwarz, & Stone, 2004). Reporting globally that one does not enjoy time with their children would likely be in stark contrast to their self-perception as a loving parent, however, reporting that on this 1 day they did not enjoy time with their children does not preclude them as quality parents. Aggregating across multiple daily reports would, therefore, reflect the parents' actual enjoyment during this time period and individual differences among parents would be based on actual differences in enjoyment rather than differences in global self-perception. Other undesirable behaviors have found similar patterns. In a study of unsafe sexual practices, it was found that participants underreported the number of unsafe sexual behaviors in general cross-sectional measures compared to daily reports (McAuliffe, DiFranceisco, & Reed, 2007).

Contrary to undesirable behaviors, global measures of life satisfaction are often negatively skewed (Diener, 2000), with most people considering themselves to be generally quite satisfied with their life. However, these responses are more likely based on their perception of themselves as a happy person, rather than on actual accounts of how satisfied they are day in and day out. Thus, aggregating over many closely spaced assessments may provide an account of an individual's true level of a construct that is less dependent on retrospection and social desirability biases.

Sampling many points in time also addresses a number of the issues that plague cross-sectional measures. Intensive measurement designs, with frequent closely spaced assessments (e.g., daily diary, ecological momentary assessments), enable within-person variation to be disaggregated from between-person differences. Furthermore, the lag-time between the experiencing and the reporting can be reduced to the point where retrospection bias is nearly eliminated and reports are based more on a bottom-up report of actual events rather than a top-down representation of perceived self-image. However, sampling time more frequently produces additional challenges. As the time-scale varies, the process that is being measured may also change in terms of quantitative or qualitative shifts (Birren & Schroots, 1996; Martin & Hofer, 2004). It cannot be assumed that constructs are equivalent across occasions or levels of analysis. Measures designed to capture stable between-person differences may not possess suitable sensitivity to accurately capture small increments in within-person variation.

Reactivity in Studies of Within-Person Change

Individuals often perform better on measures of performance and functional assessments with repeated testing, with the greatest gains following the first assessment. This phenomenon is known as retest, practice, exposure, learning, or reactivity, and has been reported in a number of longitudinal studies of aging (Ferrer, Salthouse, Stewart, & Schwartz, 2004; Hultsch, Hertzog, Dixon, & Small, 1998; Rabbitt, Diggle, Smith, Holland, & Mc Innes, 2001; Schaie, 1996). A further complication is that individuals are likely to differ from one another in terms of amount of gain due to retesting or learning in systematic ways related to age or developmental stage, level of ability or age and test-specific learning, such as learning content and strategies. Additionally, such gains may be due to underperformance at the first occasion, known as warm-up effects and related to initial anxiety. Sliwinski, Hoffman, and Hofer (2010) addressed retest effects in a longitudinal design based on measurement bursts, a set of closely spaced retest intervals to model practice effects and longer, for example, 6-month intervals to model age-related changes (Nesselroade, 1991). The pairing of multi-burst designs and informative measurement models allowed the separation of short-term (e.g., retest gains) from longtime developmental change, which operate across two different time scales.

OPTIMIZING MEASUREMENT FOR BETWEEN-PERSON DIFFERENCES AND WITHIN-PERSON CHANGE AND VARIATION

Measurements that are developed for between-person differences may not be optimal for within-person research. Intensive measurement designs are now commonly utilized to account for within-person variation (e.g., Bolger & Laurenceau, 2013; Rush & Grouzet, 2012; Sliwinski, Smyth, Hofer, & Stawski, 2006), where either new measures are created to be used in these designs, or more commonly, are adapted from measures designed for between-person cross-sectional research. Though these new measures may be a better solution to account for within-person variation, little effort has been devoted to evaluating the properties of these measures to adequately account for within-person variation and between-person difference. The structure, reliability, and validity of measures used in intensive measurement designs need to be evaluated with the same rigor that is expected of cross-sectional measures. Multilevel reliability estimates and factor analysis allow for these measurement properties to be readily examined. Here, we illustrate a number of measurement challenges and innovations in measurement development.

Alternative Measurement Models Based on Intensive Measurement Designs

Sample data from a daily diary study of 147 participants ($M_{age} = 20$) assessed over 14 consecutive days on measures of subjective well-being (i.e., life satisfaction, positive and negative affect) will be used to demonstrate how intensive measurement designs, which emphasize within-person measurement, can be utilized to generate a between-person measure that may be preferred over cross-sectional measures. Participants initially completed global cross-sectional measures of the 5-item Satisfaction with Life Scale (SWLS; Pavot & Diener, 1993) and the 20-item Positive and Negative Affect Schedule (PANAS; Watson, Clark, & Tellegen, 1988). The same scales were adapted slightly to be used for daily assessments and were administered over the next 14 days to capture daily levels of life satisfaction, positive affect (PA), and negative affect (NA).

The daily measures of well-being possessed considerable amounts of within-person variability. Intraclass correlation coefficients (ICC), which indicate the proportion of variability that is between-person, were around 0.5 for all three measures (see Table 1). Thus, half of the total variability was due to within-person variation, such that individuals deviated as much from their own mean level of well-being as their own mean deviated from the grand mean (see Figure 2). Relying solely on a cross-sectional measure would ignore all within-person variability and assume that these constructs were stable across time. Furthermore, all within-person variability would be confounded with between-person variability, impacting the conclusions drawn at a between-person level. Disaggregating within- and between-person variability

TABLE 1

RELIABILITY ESTIMATES (ω) COMPARING CROSS-SECTIONAL MEASURES AND DAILY MEASURES OF WELL-BEING

Variable	Cross-Sectional Measure			Daily Measure					
	M	SD	Omega (BP)	M	SD	Omega (BP)	Omega (WP)	ICC	r
Life satisfaction	4.33	0.82	0.789	3.56	0.91	0.970	0.855	0.53	0.58
Positive affect	3.53	0.65	0.862	2.77	0.55	0.956	0.844	0.45	0.51
Negative affect	1.98	0.65	0.804	1.61	0.48	0.966	0.823	0.48	0.54

Note. BP = between-person; WP = within-person; ICC = intraclass correlation coefficient; r = correlation between cross-sectional and daily measure.

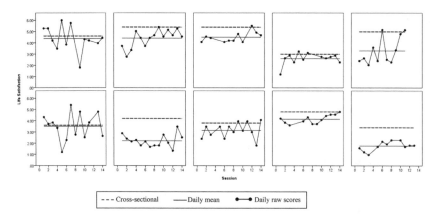

--- Cross-sectional   —— Daily mean   ●—● Daily raw scores

Figure 2.—Reported life satisfaction values from ten random participants displaying differences in cross-sectional, aggregated daily mean, and daily raw score measures.

allows the effects at both levels to be more appropriately modeled and accounted for.

As outlined above, the cross-sectional measures are more susceptible to retrospection and social desirability biases than the daily measures. This would be expected especially for the global measure of life satisfaction, where individuals tend to view themselves in an overly positive light on global measures. Comparing the cross-sectional measure of life satisfaction to the aggregated daily measure reveals that the two measures are only moderately correlated ($r = 0.58$, Table 1). Additionally, individuals rated their general level of life satisfaction higher than their average daily life satisfaction [$t(146) = 11.71$, $p < .001$]. Figure 2 shows the comparison of the cross-sectional and daily measures of 10 participants. Each participant had higher levels on the cross-sectional life satisfaction measure than the aggregated daily measure. More than 85% of the sample overestimated their global life satisfaction relative to their daily mean, providing support for the upward bias of cross-sectional measures. When reporting on typical level of life satisfaction, participants were likely using a top-down approach where they perceived themselves as more satisfied to a greater extent than was actually the case if asked to assess day-by-day. It is important to note that global perceptions of life satisfaction may be of substantive interest, however, it differs from actual experiences of life satisfaction as they occur on a daily basis.

In addition to disaggregating effects and reducing bias, repeated measurements improve the reliability of between-person estimates (Sliwinski, 2008). Calculation of reliability is often neglected in within-person measurements, or a single-level alpha is reported that does not account for the hierarchical data structure. Recent work on multilevel reliability provides practical alternatives to single-level reliability estimates (e.g., Cranford et al., 2006; Geldhof, Preacher, & Zyphur, 2014; Shrout & Lane, 2012). We suggest utilizing a multilevel omega (ω) reliability estimate derived from multilevel confirmatory factor analysis (CFA) that was outlined by Geldhof et al. (2014) (see also McDonald, 1999; Shrout & Lane, 2012). The ω reliability utilizes the factor loadings to derive the ratio of true score variance to total variance:

$$\omega = \frac{\left(\Sigma \lambda_i\right)^2}{\left(\Sigma \lambda_i\right)^2 + \Sigma \Psi_i^2}, \tag{1}$$

where λ_i and Ψ_i^2 are the factor loading and residual variance for item i, respectively. This equation can be applied to both levels of the multilevel factor model to derive both within- and between-person reliability. Table 1 displays the multilevel reliability estimates for the daily measures and the single-level (between-person) reliability estimate for the cross-sectional measure. It is clear that between-person reliability is improved considerably by employing an intensive measurement design over a cross-sectional (single-occasion) design.

Multilevel Factor Analysis: Evaluation of Structure at Between- and Within-Person Levels
Intensive repeated measure designs allow for both a within- and between-person factor structure to be examined simultaneously through the use of multilevel factor analysis. In multilevel factor analysis, the within-person factor structure reflects common covariance in the indicators at each specific occasion, pooled across occasions and individuals. The between-person factor structure reflects common covariance in individual levels of indicators aggregated across time (i.e., person-mean level). Similar to conventional factor analysis, the quality of the model can be assessed with a variety of fit indices, which include both global fit indices (e.g., comparative fit index [CFI], root mean square error of approximation [RMSEA]) and level-specific fit indices (e.g., standardized root mean square residual [SRMR] within/between).

Multilevel confirmatory factor analyses were employed in Mplus v.7 (Muthén & Muthén, 2012) to evaluate the optimal within-person and between-person factor structure of the SWLS (see Appendix for sample Mplus code). Multilevel CFA allows for the within-person variance to be disaggregated from the between-person variance, while still attenuating for measurement error at both levels. The multilevel measurement model can be expressed by the following equation (Muthén, 1991; Preacher, Zyphur, & Zhang, 2010):

$$Y_{ij} = v + \lambda_w \eta_{ij} + \varepsilon_{ij} + \lambda_b \eta_i + \varepsilon_i, \tag{2}$$

where Y_{ij} is a p-dimensional vector of observed variables for individual i on occasion j, where p is the number of observed indicators; v is a p-dimensional vector of intercepts; λ_w is a $p \times q$ within-person factor loadings matrix, where q is the number of latent variables; λ_b is a $p \times q$ between-person factor loadings matrix; η_{ij} and η_i are q-dimensional vectors of within-person and between-person latent variables, respectively; and ε_{ij} and ε_i are p-dimensional vectors of within-person and between-person specific factors (i.e., residuals), respectively. At the between-person level, the indicators are person means of each within-person indicator that are aggregated in order to adjust for unreliability in sampling error (see Lüdtke et al., 2008, for further details), such that the between-person indicators are represented as latent means.

In the case of the SWLS, a single factor at both the within- and between-person level fit the data extremely well, with all five items loading onto this single factor (see Table 2; Figure 3). These five items reliably covary within a person across occasions (i.e., on occasions when one item deviates from typical levels, the other four items also deviate in the same direction) and between people (i.e., individuals who are higher on one item relative to others are also higher on the other items). It will not always be the case that the

TABLE 2

Standardized Factor Loadings From Multilevel Confirmatory Factor Analyses of the Daily Measures of Life Satisfaction and Competence

Multilevel Factor Models	ICC	Factor Loadings	
		WP	BP
Life satisfaction[a]			
LS1	0.51	0.82	0.99
LS2	0.51	0.72	0.90
LS3	0.50	0.80	0.94
LS4	0.29	0.64	0.78
LS5	0.48	0.75	0.98
Factor variance	0.61	1.766	2.751
Competence[b]			
Comp1	0.33	0.63	0.88
Comp2	0.29	0.34	0.16
Comp3	0.36	0.73	0.96
Comp4	0.38	0.63	0.89
Comp5	0.30	0.33	−0.05
Comp6	0.34	0.54	0.33
Comp7	0.41	0.70	0.96
Factor variance	0.49	1.107	1.052

Note. LS = life satisfaction; Comp = competence; ICC = intraclass correlation coefficient; WP = within-person; BP = between-person.
[a]$\chi^2(10) = 15.83$, CFI $= 0.997$, SRMR(WP) $= 0.01$, SRMR(BP) $= 0.02$, RMSEA $= 0.02$.
[b]$\chi^2(28) = 256.44$, CFI $= 0.89$, SRMR(WP) $= 0.04$, SRMR(BP) $= 0.21$, RMSEA $= 0.07$.

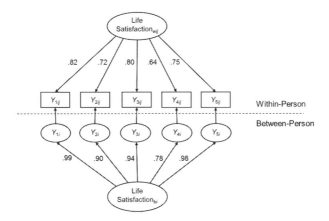

FIGURE 3.—Multilevel confirmatory factor model of life satisfaction with one within-person factor and one between-person factor.

within-person structure is identical to the between-person structure. For example, Rush and Hofer (2014) found that the PANAS was best represented by two inversely related factors (PA and NA) at the within-person level, but independent PA and NA factors at the between-person level.

Discrepancies in model fit across levels demand additional decisions. Situations where the measure fits well at the within-person level, but not at the between-person level, require decisions to be made about the utility of the measure and the appropriateness for assessing between-person differences. For example, a 7-item daily measure of competence that was adapted from the cross-sectional measure of psychological well-being (Ryff, 1989) was also included in the above sample data. Results from a multilevel CFA revealed good model fit at the within-person level (SRMR = .04; with all items loading onto a single factor), but not at the between-person (SRMR = .21; see Table 2). Specifically, items 2 and 5 did not load well onto the between-person factor of competence (loadings = .16 and −.05, respectively), but did load onto the within-person factor (loading = .34 and .33, respectively). In this situation, the same scale may not capture both within-person variation and between-person differences with the same precision and accuracy and decisions will depend on the intended use of the scale (i.e., to capture characteristic individual levels or intraindividual variations). The goal may be to develop scales that adequately measure both within- and between-person elements. However, depending on the constructs of interest, this may not always be feasible as they may manifest themselves differently across levels of analysis. Multilevel factor analysis provides a technique to evaluate the multilevel structure of measures to ensure they adequately reflect the constructs they are intended. This technique further enables the reliability and validity to be examined across levels. A greater emphasis on the measurement properties from multilevel data will go a long way in enhancing the quality of measures, and as a result the conclusions drawn from them.

Trait as Maximal Performance (e.g., Cognition)

Aggregation of frequent repeated measurements may not always be the optimal approach to capture an individual's characteristic level. For measures of cognitive or physical ability, repeated assessments will often lead to improvements in performance related to learning content, strategies, or due to repeated practice or training gains. This modification of the system itself that result in improved or altered performance on subsequent assessments is an important consideration in longitudinal developmental research. For example, in the case of executive functioning, as a consequence of repeated assessment and learning the problem-solving strategy, over time the test may measure a different construct than it did originally, particularly when the test was designed to measure novel reasoning ability. In many cases, however, such retest effects can be managed through the use of a measurement burst design, permitting the estimation of maximal performance and change in maximal performance over time (Sliwinski et al., 2010; see also Hoffman, Hofer, & Sliwinski, 2011; Thorvaldsson, Hofer, Berg, & Johansson, 2006, for critique of other approaches for correcting for retest effects).

Optimizing Assessments: Planned Missingness Designs, Adaptive Tests, and Web-Based Assessment

To be able to appropriately model within- and between-person constructs a sufficient number of items and measurement occasions are often required. However, large item scales assessed frequently over many occasions can become burdensome on participants. Among the most frequently criticized elements of daily diary studies that participants complain about is the repetitiveness of the questionnaires. An approach to minimize the repetitiveness, while still ensuring enough items to appropriately capture and evaluate the constructs through multilevel CFAs, could utilize a planned missingness design (e.g., Graham, Hofer, & MacKinnon, 1996; McArdle, 1994; Silvia, Kwapil, Walsh, & Myin-Germeys, 2014). Planned missingness designs present a few anchor items at each occasion, while presenting a remaining set of items intermittently over the course of the assessment period. In this way, participants are presented with some different items each occasion, which enhances their interest and motivation to continue. These designs also reduce the total number of items that are required to be asked at each occasion, allowing for a greater number of overall constructs to be examined, without the risk of burning out the participants. Furthermore, the rotating items can still be included within a multilevel SEM framework to evaluate the fit, reliability, and validity of the constructs.

Adaptive testing can serve a similar purpose for cognitive and performance testing that the planned missingness design serves for survey measures. Adaptive tests that adjust to the participants ability level provide a way for the participant to reach their maximal performance level in fewer trials or items than standard tests (Gorin & Embretson, 2012). The reduced time of each test reduces the burden and fatigue on the participants and allows for more assessments and/or greater depth or range of constructs (e.g., cognition, psychopathology, affect, behavioral dispositions) to be evaluated at each assessment (Kim-O & Embretson, 2010).

Developing novel approaches to reduce the time and burden on the participants without sacrificing the necessity for quality of measures will be paramount in the development of measures that adequately capture both within-person change and variation and between-person differences in these dynamic processes. The growing availability of web-based and mobile assessment tools will enable data to be collected more readily in remote locations (i.e., the participant's home; Intille, 2007). As intensive measurement designs become less burdensome and costly for participants and researchers, the benefits will clearly outweigh the costs. However, in order to ensure that these designs are utilized to their potential, a greater focus must be placed on developing measures that adequately and appropriately capture both within-person variation and between-person differences.

SUMMARY AND CLOSING STATEMENT

An increasing number of research studies demonstrate the remarkable intraindividual variability that is present in cognitive, behavioral, and physical functioning across different time scales. The results from these studies, and that of several measurement studies using short-term repeated assessments, provide evidence that single assessments do not usually provide optimal estimates of an average or typical value of a person's functioning, and adversely affect results from between- and within-person analysis. We have highlighted the strengths of measuring individuals more often in order to better sample the contextual and intrinsic variation of individual functioning. As we make use of existing measures and adapt them for repeated-measures designs, we are finding that some of these measures may not be optimal for such purposes. There is a need for developing measures that are sufficiently sensitive for detecting within-person variation and change. Such developments have the potential to improve measures and models of between-person differences and to understand whether such measurements can be homogeneously applied to all individuals within a population. We demonstrated how measuring individuals more often can improve the discrimination of between-person differences by disentangling true between-person differences in typical level from contextual and/or intrinsic intra-individual variation. Such designs encourage us to make our assessments more efficient and less burdensome, such as through planned missingness designs, adaptive tests, and web-based assessment.

REFERENCES

Allen, J. P., Chango, J., Szwedo, D., Schad, M., & Marston, E. (2012). Predictors of susceptibility to peer influence regarding substance use in adolescence. *Child Development*, **83**, 337–350.

Barta, W. D., Tennen, H., & Litt, M. D. (2012). Measurement reactivity in diary research. In M. R. Mehl & T. S. Conner (Eds.), *Handbook of research methods for studying daily life* (pp. 108–123). New York, NY: Guilford Press.

Birren, J. E., & Schroots, J. J. F. (1996). History, concepts, and theory in the psychology of aging. In J. E. Birren, K. W. Schaie, R. P. Abeles, M. Gatz, & T. A. Salthouse (Eds.), *Handbook of the psychology of aging* (4th ed., pp. 3–23). San Diego, CA: Academic Press.

Bolger, N., & Laurenceau, J. P. (2013). *Intensive longitudinal methods: An introduction to diary and experience sampling research*. New York, NY: Guilford Press.

Bontempo, D. E., Grouzet, F. M. E., & Hofer, S. M. (2012). Measurement issues in the analysis of within-person change. In J. T. Newsom, R. N. Jones, & S. M. Hofer (Eds.), *Longitudinal data analysis: A practical guide for researchers in aging, health, and social sciences* (pp. 97–142). New York, NY: Routledge.

Bontempo, D. E., & Hofer, S. M. (2007). Assessing factorial invariance in cross-sectional and longitudinal studies. In A. D. Ong & M. H. M. van Dulmen (Eds.), *Oxford handbook of methods in positive psychology* (pp. 153–175). New York, NY: Oxford University Press.

Cranford, J. A., Shrout, P. E., Iida, M., Rafaeli, E., Yip, T., & Bolger, N. (2006). A procedure for evaluating sensitivity to within-person change: Can mood measures in diary studies detect change reliably? *Personality and Social Psychology Bulletin*, **32**, 917–929.

Curran, P. J., & Bauer, D. J. (2011). The disaggregation of within-person and between-person effects in longitudinal models of change. *Annual Review of Psychology*, **62**, 583–619.

Diener, E. (2000). Subjective well-being: The science of happiness and a proposal for a national index. *American Psychologist*, **55**, 34–43.

Ferrer, E., Balluerka, N., & Widaman, K. F. (2008). Factorial invariance and the specification of second-order latent growth models. *Methodology*, **4**, 22–36.

Ferrer, E., Salthouse, T. A., Stewart, W. F., & Schwartz, B. S. (2004). Modeling age and retest processes in longitudinal studies of cognitive abilities. *Psychology and Aging*, **19**, 243–259.

Geldhof, G. J., Preacher, K. J., & Zyphur, M. J. (2014). Reliability estimation in a multilevel confirmatory factor analysis framework. *Psychological Methods*, **19**, 72–91.

Gorin, J. S., & Embretson, S. E. (2012). Using cognitive psychology to generate items and predict item characteristics. In M. J. Gierl & T. M. Haladyna (Eds.), *Automatic item generation: Theory and practice* (pp. 136–156). New York, NY: Taylor & Francis.

Graham, J. W., Hofer, S. M., & MacKinnon, D. P. (1996). Maximizing the usefulness of data obtained with planned missing value patterns: An application of maximum likelihood procedures. *Multivariate Behavioral Research*, **31**, 197–218.

Hoffman, L. (2007). Multilevel models for examining individual differences in within-person variation and covariation over time. *Multivariate Behavioral Research*, **42**, 609–629.

Hoffman, L., Hofer, S. M., & Sliwinski, M. J. (2011). On the confounds among retest gains and age-cohort differences in the estimation of within-person change in longitudinal studies: A simulation study. *Psychology and Aging*, **26**, 778–791.

Hoffman, L., & Stawski, R. S. (2009). Persons as contexts: Evaluating between-person and within-person effects in longitudinal analysis. *Research in Human Development*, **6**, 97–120.

Hultsch, D. F., Hertzog, C., Dixon, R. A., & Small, B. J. (1998). *Memory change in the aged.* Cambridge, MA: Cambridge University Press.

Intille, S. S. (2007). Technological innovations enabling automatic, context-sensitive ecological momentary assessment. In A. A. Stone, S. Shiffman, A. A. Atienza, & L. Nebeling (Eds.), *The science of real-time data capture: Self-report in health research* (pp. 308–337). New York, NY: Oxford University Press.

Jordan, L. P., & Graham, E. (2012). Resilience and well-being among children of migrant parents in South-East Asia. *Child Development*, **83**, 1672–1688.

Juster, F. T. (1985). Preferences for work and leisure. In F. T. Juster & F. P. Stafford (Eds.), *Time, goods, and well-being* (pp. 335–351). Ann Arbor, MI: Institute for Social Research.

Kagan, J. (1980). Four questions in psychological development. *International Journal of Behavioral Development*, **3**, 231–241.

Kahneman, D., Krueger, A. B., Schkade, D. A., Schwarz, N., & Stone, A. A. (2004). A survey method for characterizing daily life experience: The Day Reconstruction Method. *Science*, **306**, 1776–1780.

Kim-O, M.-A., & Embretson, S. E. (2010). Item response theory and its application to measurement in behavioral medicine. In A. Steptoe (Ed.), *Handbook of behavioral medicine* (pp. 113–123). New York, NY: Springer.

Ladd, G. W., & Kochenderfer-Ladd, B. (2002). Identifying victims of peer aggression from early to middle childhood: Analysis of cross-informant data for concordance, estimation of relational adjustment, prevalence of victimization, and characteristics of identified victims. *Psychological Assessment*, **14**, 74–96.

Lerner, R. M., Schwartz, S. J., & Phelps, E. (2009). Problematics of time and timing in the longitudinal study of human development: Theoretical and methodological issues. *Human Development*, **52**, 44–68.

Lüdtke, O., Marsh, H. W., Robitzsch, A., Trautwein, U., Asparouhov, T., & Muthén, B. (2008). The multilevel latent covariate model: A new, more reliable approach to group-level effects in contextual studies. *Psychological Methods*, **13**, 203–229.

Martin, M., & Hofer, S. M. (2004). Intraindividual variability, change, and aging: Conceptual and analytical issues. *Gerontology*, **50**, 7–11.

McArdle, J. J. (1994). Structural factor analysis experiments with incomplete data. *Multivariate Behavioral Research*, **29**, 409–454.

McArdle, J. J., Grimm, K. J., Hamagami, F., Bowles, R. P., & Meredith, W. (2009). Modeling life-span growth curves of cognition using longitudinal data with multiple samples and changing scales of measurement. *Psychological Methods*, **14**, 126–149.

McAuliffe, T. L., DiFranceisco, W., & Reed, B. R. (2007). Effects of question format and collection mode on the accuracy of retrospective surveys of health risk behavior: A comparison with daily sexual activity diaries. *Health Psychology*, **26**, 60–67.

McDonald, R. P. (1999). *Test theory: A unified treatment.* Mahwah, NJ: Erlbaum.

Meredith, W., & Horn, J. (2001). The role of factorial invariance in modeling growth and change. In L. M. Collins & A. G. Sayer (Eds.), *New methods for the analysis of change* (pp. 203–240). Washington, DC: American Psychological Association.

Muthén, B. O. (1991). Multilevel factor analysis of class and student achievement components. *Journal of Educational Measurement*, **28**, 338–354.

Muthén, L. K., & Muthén, B. O. (1998–2012). *Mplus user's guide* (7th ed.) Los Angeles, CA: Muthén & Muthén.

Nesselroade, J. R. (1991). The warp and the woof of the developmental fabric. In R. M. Downs, L. S. Liben, & D. S. Palermo (Eds.), *Visions of aesthetics, the environment & development: The legacy of Joachim F. Wohlwill* (pp. 213–240). Hillsdale, NJ: Erlbaum.

Pavot, W., & Diener, E. (1993). Review of the satisfaction with life scale. *Psychological Assessment,* **5**, 164–172.

Preacher, K. J., Zyphur, M. J., & Zhang, Z. (2010). A general multilevel SEM framework for assessing multilevel mediation. *Psychological Methods,* **15**, 209–233.

Rabbitt, P., Diggle, P., Smith, D., Holland, F., & Mc Innes, L. (2001). Identifying and separating the effects of practice and of cognitive ageing during a large longitudinal study of elderly community residents. *Neuropsychologia,* **39**, 532–543.

Rast, P., & Hofer, S. M. (2014). Substantial power to detect variance and covariance among rates of change: Results based on actual longitudinal studies and related simulations. *Psychological Methods,* **19**, 133–154.

Rast, P., MacDonald, S. W., & Hofer, S. M. (2012). Intensive measurement designs for research on aging. *GeroPsych: The Journal of Gerontopsychology and Geriatric Psychiatry,* **25**, 45–55.

Rush, J., & Grouzet, F. M. E. (2012). It is about time: Daily relationships between temporal perspective and well-being. *The Journal of Positive Psychology,* **7**, 427–442.

Rush, J., & Hofer, S. M. (2014). Differences in within- and between-person factor structure of positive and negative affect: Analysis of two intensive measurement studies using multilevel structural equation modeling. *Psychological Assessment,* **20**, 462–473.

Ryff, C. D. (1989). Happiness is everything, or is it? Explorations on the meaning of psychological well-being. *Journal of Personality and Social Psychology,* **57**, 1069–1081.

Salthouse, T. A., & Nesselroade, J. R. (2010). Dealing with short-term fluctuation in longitudinal research. *The Journal of Gerontology: Psychological Sciences,* **65B**, 698–705.

Schaie, K. W. (1996). *Intellectual development in adulthood: The Seattle longitudinal study.* New York, NY: Cambridge University Press.

Schwarz, N. (2012). Why researchers should think "real-time": A cognitive rationale. In M. R. Mehl & T. S. Conner (Eds.), *Handbook of research methods for studying daily life* (pp. 22–42) New York, NY: Guilford Press.

Schwarz, N., Kahneman, D., & Xu, J. (2009). Global and episodic reports of hedonic experience. In R. Belli, F. Stafford, & D. Alwin (Eds.), *Using calendar and diary methods in life events research* (pp. 157–174). Los Angeles, CA: Sage Publications.

Schwarz, N., & Strack, F. (1999). Reports of subjective well-being: Judgmental processes and their methodological implications. In D. Kahneman, E. Diener, & N. Schwarz (Eds.), *Well-being: The foundations of hedonic psychology* (pp. 61–84). New York, NY: Russell Sage Foundation.

Shrout, P. E., & Lane, S. P. (2012). Psychometrics. In M. R. Mehl & T. S. Conner (Eds.), *Handbook of research methods for studying daily life* (pp. 302–320). New York, NY: Guilford Press.

Silvia, P. J., Kwapil, T. R., Walsh, M. A., & Myin-Germeys, I. (2014). Planned missing-data designs in experience-sampling research: Monte Carlo simulations of efficient designs for assessing within-person constructs. *Behavior Research Methods,* **46**, 41–54.

Sliwinski, M. J. (2008). Measurement-burst designs for social health research. *Social and Personality Psychology Compass,* **2**, 245–261.

Sliwinski, M. J., Hoffman, L., & Hofer, S. (2010). Modeling retest and aging effects in a measurement burst design. In P. C. M. Molenaar & K. M. Newell (Eds.), *Individual pathways of change: Statistical models for analyzing learning and development* (pp. 37–50). Washington, DC: American Psychological Association.

Sliwinski, M. J., Smyth, J. M., Hofer, S. M., & Stawski, R. S. (2006). Intraindividual coupling of daily stress and cognition. *Psychology and Aging*, **21**, 545–557.

Thorvaldsson, V., Hofer, S. M., Berg, S., & Johansson, B. (2006). Effects of repeated testing in a longitudinal age-homogeneous study of cognitive aging. *The Journal of Gerontology: Psychological Sciences*, **61B**, P348–P354.

Walls, T. A., Barta, W. D., Stawski, R. S., Collyer, C. E., & Hofer, S. M. (2012). Time-scale-dependent longitudinal designs. In B. Laursen, T. D. Little, & N. A. Card (Eds.), *Handbook of developmental research methods* (pp. 46–64). New York, NY: Guilford Press.

Watson, D., Clark, L. A., & Tellegen, A. (1988). Development and validation of brief measures of positive and negative affect: The PANAS scales. *Journal of Personality and Social Psychology*, **54**, 1063–1070.

Appendix

TITLE: Mplus code for Daily Life Satisfaction multilevel CFA;

DATA: FILE = WB_mfa_2012.dat;
    FORMAT = free;
    TYPE = INDIVIDUAL;

VARIABLE:
    NAMES ARE ID Session d_ls1 d_ls2 d_ls3 d_ls4 d_ls5;
    USEVARIABLES ARE ID d_ls1 d_ls2 d_ls3 d_ls4 d_ls5;
    MISSING ARE ALL (999);
    CLUSTER = ID;

ANALYSIS: TYPE IS TWOLEVEL;
    ESTIMATOR = MLR;

MODEL:

!!!!! Two-Level CFA: 1 within factor, 1 between factor;

!! Level-1, day-level model;
    %WITHIN%
    fw BY d_ls1 d_ls2 d_ls3 d_ls4 d_ls5;

!! Level-2, person-level model;
    %BETWEEN%
    fb BY d_ls1 d_ls2 d_ls3 d_ls4 d_ls5;

OUTPUT: Sampstat; STDYX;

VI. PERSON-SPECIFIC INDIVIDUAL DIFFERENCE APPROACHES IN DEVELOPMENTAL RESEARCH

Michael J. Rovine and Lawrence L. Lo

This article is part of the issue "Developmental Methodology" Card (Issue Author). For a full listing of articles in this issue, see: http://onlinelibrary.wiley.com/doi/10.1111/mono.v82.2/issuetoc.

In this chapter, we demonstrate the way certain common analytic approaches (e.g., polynomial curve modeling, repeated measures ANOVA, latent curve, and other factor models) create individual difference measures based on a common underlying model. After showing that these approaches require only means and covariance (or correlation) matrices to estimate regression coefficients based on a hypothesized model, we describe how to recast these models based on time-series related approaches focusing on single subject time series approaches (e.g., vector autoregressive approaches and *P-technique* factor models). We show how these latter methods create parameters based on models that can vary from individual-to-individual. We demonstrate differences for the factor model using real data examples.

An important question for researchers involved in modeling individual differences involves how a particular analytic technique results in variable values that are used to describe individuals. The emphasis on models for individuals based on the collection of more intensive data (see Rush & Hofer, Chapter 5, this volume) has led to a number of new analytic approaches often based on time series methods (Walls & Schafer, 2006). The development of methods described as person-specific has placed more emphasis on models that describe individuals. These approaches highlight the difference between nomothetic models that tend to estimate parameters based on group

Corresponding author: Michael J. Rovine, University of Pennsylvania, Philadelphia, PA; email: mrovine@upenn.edu
DOI: 10.1111/mono.12300

characteristics and idiographic models that tend to estimate a separate model for each individual (Lamiell, 1981; Zevon & Tellegen, 1982). Molenaar (2004) described the problems inherent in using group based models to describe characteristics of individuals; notably that the required assumption that a model developed on a group holds for each member of the group may not be satisfied. This requirement, related to the *ergodicity* hypothesis (Birkhoff, 1931) is a testable assumption only when the data collected for each individual is a long enough time series that both individual and group models can be estimated and compared. With fewer occasions of measurement this represents an untested assumption.

The important implication of the failure to satisfy the assumption of ergodicity is that models based on results pooled across a group may present a poor description of individuals within a group. As a result, any predictions made for an individual within that group may be invalid. Lacking time series data, this may well be another source of prediction error. With time series data, this becomes a testable assumption with the possibility of improved predictions based on the more intensive data. As technology makes the collection of more intensive data more tenable, researchers will have more opportunity to develop more person-specific models.

In this chapter, we demonstrate the way certain common analytic approaches such as longitudinal regression modeling, linear mixed modeling (e.g., curve modeling through polynomial curve parameterization and repeated measures ANOVA), and factor modeling create individual difference measures based on a common underlying model. After showing that these approaches depend on sufficient (summary) statistics and create individual parameter predictions based on an underlying assumed probability model, we compare these methods to more person-specific approaches. We focus on analogous single-subject time series approaches concentrating on vector autoregressive approaches and *P-technique* factor models, and show how these latter methods create parameters based on models that can vary from individual to individual. For the factor analytic approach, we demonstrate the problem of using a group-based model to describe characteristics of individuals using mood data (Corneal, 1990; Rovine, Molenaar, & Corneal, 1999) and personality data (Borkenau & Ostendorf, 1998) showing that the group-based model is an incorrect model when used to describe the individuals in the sample.

GROUP-BASED INDIVIDUAL DIFFERENCED MODELS

Many popular analytical methods create values for individual difference parameters based on group models. For example, the multilevel curve model (Bryk & Raudenbush, 1992; Goldstein, 1995; McArdle & Epstein, 1987;

see Grimm et al., Chapter 4, this volume) can be used to generate individual intercepts and regression slopes in addition to the group intercept and slopes that are typically the focus of the model. While the individual measures can be used to describe differences among participants in a study, they are created based on the group parameter estimates; namely, the regression weights of the model and the common covariance structure of the random effects. The individual variable values are then predicted using these group parameter values based on certain assumptions regarding the distribution of these variables (e.g., the individual values will be normally distributed with a zero mean). While this represents a perfectly reasonable way to provide these values under a particular common model, this approach represents the assumption that the same model holds for all study participants. With a relatively few number of occasions of measurement, this assumption cannot be tested. With more intensive time series data, however, this assumption can tested, and individual models can be determined. It may be the case that different individuals require different models. There may be unknown subgroups whose data may be described by a common model, but this is not known a priori. With more intensive time series data, a separate model can be determined for each study participant. Individuals with common models can then be clustered to form subgroups (Nesselroade & Molenaar, 1999).

One common model where this can become evident is the longitudinal lagged regression model based on a panel design. Here, we will show how the group-based model relates to the individual-based vector autoregressive model.

A second family of analytic procedures that we consider encompasses methods based on the linear mixed model, which include multilevel polynomial curve modeling and repeated measures ANOVA. As an example, for the linear multilevel curve model,[1] individual slopes and intercepts are generated as part of the solution. These are often interpreted as individual difference measures. They are based on post hoc predictions of the model and are common to all participants in the sense that they represent variations of a single underlying model with an attached probability distribution for the residuals (Robinson, 1991). The common underlying model makes these "individual difference" measures much different than those that would result from a separate time series model for each individual.

Another model we consider is the common factor model. The solution to the factor model is based on pooling data across individuals and analyzing the resultant correlation matrix. With a few occasions of measurement, this can be extended into the longitudinal factor model.[2] Like the common factor model, this model is the result of a *subjects* × *variables* data set where the variables for the different occasions are the variables of the model. As a result, this is still a group-based model as the correlation is once again pooled across subjects.

As an alternative, we will consider a factor analysis based on collecting multiple *variables* on multiple *occasions* on a single *subject*. Here, *occasions* essentially takes the place of *subjects*. A correlation (or covariance) matrix can be constructed with such data, and, as a result, individual factor models can be estimated. The factor loadings and factor correlations of these different individual models can be compared both to each other and to results of the group-based *subjects* × *variables* results, which provides a test of the *ergodicity* hypothesis; namely, does the group-based model describe what happens to each of the individuals? We will demonstrate how individual models can differ from the group model using data from Rovine et al. (1999) and Borkenau and Ostendorf (1998).

Other modeling approaches attempt to account for heterogeneity of intraindividual variation in creating individual difference parameters. Latent class trajectory analysis (Nagin, 1999) and growth-mixture modeling (Muthén & Shedden, 1999) create subgroups by implicitly clustering individuals with similar predicted parameter values. Although these methods allow heterogeneity in terms of differences in the predicted parameter values, there will still be strong distribution assumptions within subgroups (Sterba & Bauer, 2010). For example, a particular subgroup within a growth mixture model will have a specified mean and covariance structure that assumes homogeneity within that subgroup. These types of models still require a common group model of which the individual parameters represent instances of that model though with wider variation across subgroups. By requiring the common model, these approaches still assume *ergodicity*.

Lagged Regression Models

As an example of a lagged regression, we consider the cross-lagged regression model with two variables, x and y, each measured on four occasions with the assumption that for person, i, at time t, $x_{i,t}$ at each occasion predicts

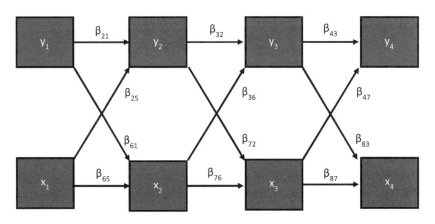

FIGURE 1.—A lagged regression model.

$y_{i,t+1}$ at the next occasion, and in turn, $y_{i,t}$ at each occasion predicts $x_{i,t+1}$ at the next occasion (Kenny, 2005). The model for such data is shown in Figure 1. Given any path model, the set of regression equations that result is given by the set of tracing rules (Wright, 1934). Simply stated, each variable in the model is a dependent variable in its own regression equation. Predictor variables for that equation are connected via one-headed arrows. Two-headed arrows represent correlations[3] or covariances (depending on the scaling) between variables. An error is linked to a particular dependent variable through a one-headed arrows. To simplify the figures, we do not include errors in the models as shown.[4] We also do not include any concurrent regression relationships.

The set of regression equations resulting from the model in Figure 1 is

$$\widehat{y}_2 = \beta_{21}y_1 + \beta_{25}x_1$$
$$\widehat{y}_3 = \beta_{32}y_2 + \beta_{36}x_2$$
$$\widehat{y}_4 = \beta_{43}y_3 + \beta_{47}x_3$$
$$\widehat{x}_2 = \beta_{61}y_1 + \beta_{65}x_1 \tag{1}$$
$$\widehat{x}_3 = \beta_{72}y_2 + \beta_{76}x_2$$
$$\widehat{x}_4 = \beta_{83}y_3 + \beta_{87}x_3$$

where in each equation, the predicted value of the dependent variable in a particular equation is represent by either $\widehat{y}$ or $\widehat{x}$. β represents a regression coefficient where the first index is the dependent variable and the second is the independent variable (Note: y_1–y_4 are indexed as variables 1 through 4 in the regression weights; x_1–x_4 are indexed as variables 5 through 8).

To estimate the regression coefficients we can imagine running six different regression models, though this can be accomplished in a single step using structural equations modeling software such as LISREL (Joreskog & Sorbom, 1996). which only requires an association matrix; either a correlation matrix, a covariance matrix, or a sums of squares and crossproducts (SSCP) matrix, depending on the degree of standardization the investigator wants in the parameter estimates. Since the regression weights are based on, for example, the correlation matrix calculated for the whole sample, these parameter estimates are group-based, not individual-based.

The Vector Autoregression Model

We now present the person-specific analog of the cross-lagged regression model. Here, we consider two time series, x and y, measure on a single subject. We hypothesize that x_t predicts y_{t+1} and y_t predicts x_{t+1}. This model appears in Figure 2.

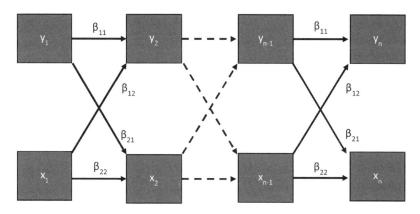

FIGURE 2.—A first-order cross-lagged vector autoregression model.

This is an example of a vector autoregression model (Lutkepohl, 2006). The model equations analogous to what we presented before are

$$\widehat{y}_{t+1} = \beta_{11}y_t + \beta_{12}x_t$$
$$\widehat{x}_{t+1} = \beta_{21}y_t + \beta_{22}x_t \qquad (2)$$

While this looks much like the cross-lagged regression model described above, here, we estimate a separate model for each individual. As a result we can put the four regression coefficients into the $\begin{bmatrix} \beta_{11} & \beta_{12} \\ \beta_{21} & \beta_{22} \end{bmatrix}$ matrix, which is person specific in that each person has their own matrix that is not dependent on other individuals' results.

By picking which regression weights we estimate we can create the analog for many different lagged regression models. For example, $\begin{bmatrix} \beta_{11} & 0 \\ 0 & \beta_{22} \end{bmatrix}$ represents the analog to the stability only model. x only predicts x and y only predicts y. This is a stability only model. If we choose to estimate $\begin{bmatrix} \beta_{11} & \beta_{12} \\ 0 & \beta_{22} \end{bmatrix}$, we are saying that x_t predicts y_{t+1}, but not the other way around. If we choose $\begin{bmatrix} \beta_{11} & 0 \\ \beta_{21} & \beta_{22} \end{bmatrix}$, the prediction is from y_t predicts x_{t+1}.

In a true individual person-specific approach we would estimate distinct models. As a result, different individuals could have different regression weights estimated. It is also possible that, for example, x_t may predict y_{t+2}, not y_{t+1}. So, in the person-specific approach, modeling would also include determining the order of autoregression for each time series and the proper order of lag. Once the proper model has been established for each individual we could determine which individuals have what models that could be described as identical. Group models could be constructed for those individuals who have identical models. Nesselroade and Molenaar (1999) have suggested methods for pooling the results of individual time series. This approach of creating samples based on the equivalence of individual models guarantees that ergodicity is satisfied and that a subgroup with an identical pooled model adequately describes each individual in the subgroup. Using such a strategy, it is most likely that different subgroups based on different (sometimes qualitatively different) models can emerge. When there are different models, the underlying process generating the series would be expected to be different for the subgroups, and this becomes an important and interesting research result. These models can, of course, easily be extended to any number of variables.

THE REGRESSION MODEL COMPOSED OF FIXED AND RANDOM EFFECTS

A typical multiple regression model could be

$$y_i = \beta_1 x_{1\,i} + \beta_2 x_{2\,i} + \beta_3 x_{3\,i} + \varepsilon_i$$

where the parameters (indicated by the Greek letters) are determined through the modeling process. In that regard, the equation can be considered to be the sum of fixed and random effects.

$$y = [\text{fixed effects}] + [\text{random effects}]$$

We identify the fixed effects as those that do not change from individual to individual. In the equation, they are indicated by regression parameters that are not indexed by i; that is, they do not change across individuals. The fixed-effect regression coefficients are β_1, β_2, and β_3. The random effects are indicated by the parameter, ε_i. This parameter is indexed by i. It changes from individual to individual. In estimating the model, the fixed effects along with the variance, σ_ε^2, of the random effects (assumed to have a particular distribution such as independent and normally distributed with mean $= 0$) are estimated as part of the regression equation. The actual values of ε_i are calculated after the fact using the observed value, y, and the predicted value of, $\hat{y}$ based on the regression equation. Generally speaking, any regression-like equation can be thought of as composed of fixed and random effects, where the fixed effects and the *covariance matrix* of the random effects are estimated as part of the model. In any group-based model, these are estimated based on the group data. Individual parameters, which for this model are the random effects, are predicted post hoc based on the parameter estimates that are the result of pooling across the group. In the person-specific model, a separate model (fixed and random effects) is estimated for each individual.

The Polynomial Curve Model

The polynomial curve model (Bryk & Raudenbush, 1992; Goldstein, 1995; McArdle & Epstein, 1987) is a member of the linear mixed-model family (Laird & Ware, 1982). To keep the discussion simple, we will assume that the shape of the curve is a straight line even though higher order polynomials may better suited to model a particular process. As the sum of fixed and random effects, the linear curve model can be conceptualized as

$$y_{\text{person } i} = [\text{group } \textit{int}\text{ercept and slope}]$$
$$+ [\text{individuals } \textit{int}\text{ercept and slope}]$$
$$+ [\text{individuals deviation from their own line}]$$

The items in the first bracket are the fixed effects; the items in the last two brackets are the random effects. As in any regression-like model, the values of the fixed effects and the covariance matrix of the random effects are estimated as part of the model. After these group-based model parameters have been determined, each individual's intercept, slope, and occasion deviations from their line can be predicted post hoc (Henderson, 1975; Robinson, 1991).

The linear curve model can be modified to include parameters that can define straight lines with different intercepts and different slopes for different groups. Curves other than straight lines can be modeled using polynomial terms (powers, centered powers, or orthogonal polynomials).

For the polynomial curve, estimating the model using the group's data becomes the requirement that the same trajectory shape describes each individual, and individuals only differ in, for example, the steepness of the slope, or the height of the intercept. When a common model does not hold, the polynomial curve approach may misrepresent how individuals differ. This may result in an inference that gives a less than optimal description about the course of change (Liu, Rovine, & Molenaar, 2012). Given the short longitudinal data that is most typically available in polynomial curve analysis, the possibility of testing to see whether the model adequately describes the sample is not available. The person-specific analog to this model would require fitting a separate polynomial to each individual. The proper order (i.e., the parameters which can describe the shape of the curve) would be empirically determined for each individual. Since with most studies, these data are not available, the polynomial curve approach often represents a necessary practical compromise.

The Data Box and Factor Analysis

In moving to a discussion of factor analysis and the differences between the grouped data and person-specific approaches, we remind the reader of the importance of the *Data Box* in conceptualizing these differences.

In his *Handbook for Multivariate Experimental Psychology*, Cattell (1966) presented a classification scheme for determining the appropriate analysis for data collected in a multivariate study. The data box, as shown in Figure 3, has three dimensions: *variables, individuals,* and *occasions.* Each two-dimensional slice or *facet* of the box represents a way of constructing an association matrix. Each possible slice can be thought of as having a dimension of interest and a dimension across which the data will be pooled. Cattell gave each two-dimension facet a letter name. For our purposes most important are the *R* and *P* facets. When interested in pooling across *individuals* to create a *variable ×* *variable* correlation matrix, one is using the *R* facet resulting in *R-technique.* This is the most common form of factor analysis. Both common cross-sectional and longitudinal factor analysis are examples of *R-technique.*

In longitudinal factor analysis (Gorsuch, 1983; Harman, 1976), the variables collected on multiple occasions are treated along the variables dimension. The data are still pooled across individuals to form a *variable by* *variable* correlation matrix. More generally, in any factor analytic model using two data box dimensions, one dimension determines the items in the

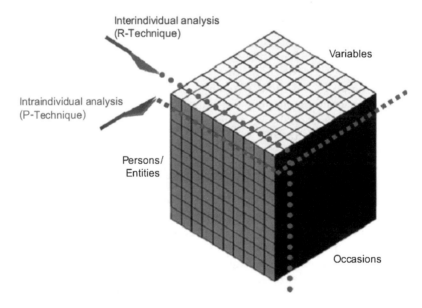

FIGURE 3.—The data box.

correlation matrix and the other dimension is what is pooled. So, in terms of longitudinal factor analysis, the *occasion* dimension is not used.[5]

For person-specific models, the *P* facet takes data for a single subject and pools across occasions to create a *variable by variable* correlation matrix. Factor analysis of this type of data set is referred to as *P-technique*. The difference between *R-* and *P-technique* is thus the dimension across which one pools based on the way data are collected, where *R-technique* pools across persons and *P-technique* pools across occasions. Both techniques are shown in the Figure 3. While others had proposed similar approaches (e.g., Stone, 1947), Cattell's factor approach has been most generally accepted.

Like the cross-sectional common factor model, the longitudinal factor model requires as input the correlation (or covariance) matrix of the input variables. These correlations are calculated for the sample and are thus based on the group. Individual values of the variables are not needed to estimate the model. The factor loadings are group-based, not person-specific. Factor scores (the individual's presumed values on the factors) are generated as post hoc predictions using a similar procedure to that of the latent curves random effects. In fact, the multilevel curve model can estimated as a constrained factor model (Rovine & Molenaar, 2000). In this form, the random effects are the factor scores of the model estimated using the fixed effects and the covariance matrix of the random effects under certain specified distributional assumptions. Despite the importance and utility of this model, it is not person-specific.

P-Technique Factor Models

As previously stated, the *ergodicity* hypothesis assumes that a group-based result can only apply to an individual when that model holds for each individual. Without true time series data that assumption cannot be tested. As Molenaar (2004) has indicated, the result of this is that cross-sectionally or longitudinally derived factor models based on a group covariance matrix can be marked different than the models that best describe each individual. As indicated above, *P-technique* factor analysis has been used to study stepchildren's emotional experiences (Corneal & Nesselroade, 1991), changes in mood (Bath, Daly, & Nesselroade, 1976), and changes in attachment security (Mitteness & Nesselroade, 1987) using essentially the standard (*R-technique*) factor analytic approach with occasions taking the place of individuals.

For the basic *P-technique* model, the data for each subject are pooled across occasions resulting in a *variable × variable* association matrix. We next demonstrate the use of a *P-technique* model first using data collected by Corneal (1990).

A Comparison of R-Technique and P-Technique Solution for the Positive and Negative Affect Scale (PANAS)

We now show how the results from *R-* and *P-technique* analysis from the same sample can differ dramatically in both the solution and the interpretation of the constructs. Rovine et al. (1999) presented data from the Positive and Negative Affect Scale (PANAS) measured on stepsons after an interaction with their stepfather. After the interaction, the child was instructed to fill out the questionnaire as soon as possible to get their immediate response to the interaction. Each child completed the items for 80 interactions resulting in a time series of length 80.

The PANAS has 20 items and was developed to have high internal consistency resulting in a hypothetical single factor. In her original study, Corneal (1990) augmented the scale with eight additional *involvement* items with the expectation that a two factor solution would result. The list of items appears in Table 1. Here, we illustrate the differences between the grouped approach represented by a cross-sectional *R-technique factor* analysis across the sample of stepchildren ($n = 29$) followed by separate *P-technique* factor analyses on three of the stepchildren.

The cross-sectional factor analysis did indeed yield a two-factor solution with a surprisingly strong simple structure. We present the *R-technique* results in Table 2. The salient factor loadings appear in bold. Positively worded items appear on *Factor 1*; negatively worded items appear on *Factor 2*. The correlation between the factors is .59 indicating that the factors share about one-third of their variance. The conclusion from this analysis is basically that the *positive* items can be used to create a positive score, the *negative* items can be used to create a negative score. Since time series data were collection (80 interactions followed by filled out the scale), we can see whether the two-factor solution holds for each person.

TABLE 1

PANAS AND INVOLVEMENT ITEMS

Distressed	Discouraged	Interested
Upset	Not Wanted	Attentive
Humiliated	Satisfied	Excited
Hostile	Content	Enthusiastic
Ashamed	Strong	Alert
Irritated	Proud	Inspired
Active	Liking	
Scared	Accepted	
Afraid	Determined	
Nervous	Closed	
Jittery	Loved	

94

TABLE 2

R-Technique Factor Analysis (Cross-Sectional) on PANAS and Involvement Items

	Factor 1	Factor 2
Inter-factor correlations		
Factor 1	1.00	0.59
Factor 2	0.59	1.00
Rotated factor pattern (standardized regression coefficients)		
Interest	**0.78**	0.07
Distressed	−0.02	**0.94**
Liking	**0.80**	−0.06
Upset	−0.18	**0.94**
Strong	**0.79**	0.13
Excited	**0.80**	0.06
Humiliated	0.23	**0.77**
Scared	0.20	**0.78**
Hostile	0.13	**0.80**
Enthusiastic	**0.90**	−0.02
Irritated	−0.01	**0.91**
Discouraged	0.01	**0.90**
Accepted	**0.85**	−0.06
Ashamed	−0.01	**0.88**
Inspired	**0.84**	0.04
Not wanted	0.01	**0.80**
Loved	**0.63**	0.13
Nervous	0.16	**0.78**
Determinde	**0.71**	0.25
Alert	**0.87**	0.03
Attentive	**0.85**	0.06
Closed	**0.79**	0.03
Satisfied	**0.82**	0.02
Proud	**0.88**	0.02
Jittery	0.16	**0.84**
Active	**0.78**	0.14
Afraid	0.06	**0.89**
Content	**0.84**	0.01

Note. The salient factor loadings appear in bold.

We next present the results for two stepchildren. We will then summarize the results for the sample.

The results for Stepson 1 appear in Table 3. Using standard criteria for determining the number of factors, a five-factor solution consistently appeared to be the best for these data. We notice that the factor correlations were all small indicating relatively independent factors. Notice also that the factor solution is more nuanced. Since the loadings tend to reflect which items co-occur, we see some interesting combinations of variables. Looking at Factors 4 and 5 we see that when the child is feeling *humiliated*, he is also feeling *unloved*. When the

TABLE 3

P-*TECHNIQUE* FACTOR ANALYSIS FOR STEPSON 1

	Factor 1	Factor 2	Factor 3	Factor 4	Factor 5
Inter-factor correlations					
Factor 1	1.00	0.13	0.18	0.02	0.11
Factor 2	0.13	1.00	0.15	−0.15	−0.35
Factor 3	0.18	0.15	1.00	−0.20	0.08
Factor 4	0.02	−0.15	−0.20	1.00	−0.05
Factor 5	0.11	−0.35	0.08	−0.05	1.00
Rotated factor pattern (standardized regression coefficients)					
Interest	0.05	**0.71**	−0.06	−0.12	0.19
Distressed	**0.85**	0.03	0.06	0.08	−0.07
Liking	−0.27	0.02	0.11	−0.09	**−0.56**
Upset	**0.77**	0.01	−0.06	0.41	0.01
Strong	**0.41**	**0.38**	0.22	0.17	−0.21
Excited	0.15	**0.68**	−0.08	−0.01	−0.00
Humiliated	0.33	0.11	0.04	**0.68**	0.03
Scared	0.01	−0.21	**0.82**	0.02	−0.38
Hostile	**0.92**	0.03	−0.16	−0.22	0.02
Enthusiastic	−0.15	**0.69**	−0.21	0.01	−0.01
Irritated	**0.87**	−0.03	−0.10	0.24	0.01
Discouraged	**0.71**	−0.02	0.24	−0.10	0.10
Accepted	**−0.51**	**0.43**	−0.07	−0.15	−0.01
Ashamed	−0.16	0.09	0.29	0.03	**0.73**
Inspired	−0.32	**0.49**	−0.04	0.11	0.09
Not wanted	0.97	−0.01	−0.15	−0.15	0.01
Loved	0.07	0.09	−0.01	**−0.57**	−0.04
Nervous	−0.16	0.05	**0.93**	0.06	0.12
Determined	**0.49**	**0.47**	0.07	−0.13	−0.06
Alert	0.19	**0.58**	0.25	0.01	0.01
Attentive	0.17	**0.66**	0.23	0.02	0.01
Closed	−0.25	0.24	0.10	−0.22	−0.33
Satisfied	**−0.45**	**0.54**	−0.01	0.11	−0.18
Proud	−0.22	**0.62**	−0.10	0.01	−0.02

Note. The salient factor loadings appear in bold.

child *dislikes* the stepparent, he tends to feel *ashamed*. Remember that the variables in each of these pairs loaded on different factors in the pooled cross-sectional solution. Looking at Factor 3, when the child is *scared*, he tends to be *nervous*. While Factors 1 and 2 tend to reflect some of the structure of the cross-sectional positive and negative factors, some important items from those original factors have split off and combined with variables from the other factor to show how this child differs from the group.

The solution for Stepson 2 appears in Table 4. Stepson 2 had a two-factor solution, but the solution differed markedly from the group solution. The

TABLE 4

P-Technique Factor Analysis for Stepson 2

	Factor 1	Factor 2
Inter-factor correlations		
Factor 1	1.00	−0.45
Factor 2	−0.45	1.00
Rotated factor pattern (standardized regression coefficients)		
Interest	**0.65**	0.10
Distressed	−0.23	**0.77**
Liking	0.20	**−0.50**
Upset	−0.37	**0.60**
Strong	**0.69**	−0.06
Excited	**0.83**	0.06
Humiliated	**−0.49**	0.05
Scared	0.25	**0.70**
Hostile	**−0.45**	**0.53**
Enthusiastic	**0.80**	−0.02
Irritated	**−0.63**	0.31
Discouraged	−0.28	**0.49**
Accepted	**0.52**	−0.27
Ashamed	0.10	**0.52**
Inspired	**0.74**	−0.00
Not wanted	**−0.57**	0.21
Loved	0.11	**−0.36**
Nervous	0.43	**0.70**
Determined	**0.64**	0.12
Alert	**0.85**	0.17
Attentive	**0.80**	0.16
Closed	0.11	−0.29
Satisfied	**0.70**	−0.12
Proud	**0.77**	0.13
Jittery	0.24	0.30
Active	**0.75**	0.09
Afraid	−0.22	**0.43**
Content	**0.56**	−0.18

Note. The salient factor loadings appear in bold.

factors are a mix of positive and negative characteristics basically scrambling the two-factor solution computed on the group. In addition, some of the variables have small enough variances that they did not correlation with any of the other variables for the reason of attenuated variance.

The number of factors differed from stepson-to-stepson. Table 5 indicates the number of how many children had a particular number of factors. Given these results, we might conclude that the two-factor positive item/negative item group solution is a relatively poor model for almost all of the participants in this study. We think it is safe to say that the factor solutions were as different

TABLE 5

The Frequency Distribution of the Number of Stepchild Factors Based on *P-Technique*

Number of Factors	Frequency
1	1
2	8
3	2
4	3
5	12
6	2
7	1
Total	29

as the children in this study. These results also demonstrate that for these data, the ergodicity assumption, namely, that the group model adequately describes each individual, is not supported.

In the exploratory factor model we presented above, each factor predicts each observed variable. We decide which variables load on which factors (are predicted by them) by the size of the regression weights or *loadings*. For each observed variable, if a regression weight is large for one factor and small for the other, we say that variable loads on that factor. An important difference between the exploratory and the confirmatory approach is that in the latter, we can hypothesize or restrict which factors predict which observed variables. We can accomplish this by fixing certain factor loadings to 0, estimating the nonfixed regression weights and then determining whether that solution can adequately reproduce the correlation matrix of the variables with the quality of the reproduction known as the fit of the model.

The Borkenau and Ostendorf Personality Data Set

Next, we demonstrate an instance of that situation of a violation of ergodicity assumption for personality factors based on the Big 5 using a data set provided by Borkenau and Ostendorf (1998). This data set included 22 individuals followed on a daily basis over 90 days with 30 personality items being repeatedly measured. The participants were psychology students from the University of Halle, Germany; course credit was given for participation. The sample consisted of 19 women and 3 men who were mostly 19 years old or in their early twenties except for three females who were in their thirties or forties. In the current example, an exploratory factor analysis is carried out at both the cross-sectional group level (*R-technique*) and for several individuals at the person-specific time-series level (*P-technique*).

An initial step in exploratory factor analysis is to determine the number of factors or latent variables that underlie a set of observed variables. In this example, we see an inconsistency in the number of factors determined via *R-* and *P-technique.* Figure 4 depicts a comparison of scree plots with the *R-technique* solution and several *P-technique* solutions. A scree plot is a visual guide for determining the number of factors, where plot points represent ordered eigenvalues that incrementally improve the explanation of a covariance structure. A scree can guide a researcher by indicating a point where a sufficient number of factors or components can be chosen; this point is usually depicted by an "elbow" in the scree. One can observe such an elbow occurring at the fourth component in the group-level scree, the second or fourth for person-A, the third for person-B, and the second, third, or fourth for person-C.

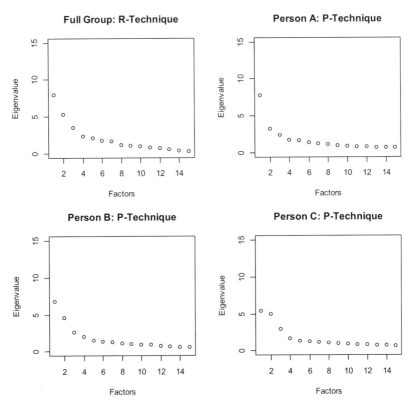

Figure 4.—A comparison of scree plots for determining the number of factors in exploratory factor analysis. The upper-left panel includes the cross-sectional group level *R-technique* analysis. The remaining plots are from randomly chosen *P-technique* analyses. The acceleration factor (AF) method indicates that that the full group suggests three factors, person-A has one factor, and persons B and C both have two factors.

In addition to the visual guide of the scree, several numerical criteria exist for determining an optimal number of factors. The acceleration factor (AF; Raiche, Riopel, & Blais, 2006), which has demonstrated satisfactory performance in both *R*- and *P-technique* was used to compare the group- and individual-level solutions. The AF is based on approximations of the second derivatives of the scree plot and similarly attempts to identify an "elbow" point by numerical methods. The AF method indicates that the group-level analysis yields a three-factor solution, person-A a one-factor solution, and both person-B and -C having a two-factor solution. These roughly correspond to the visually identified "elbow" points within the scree plots as indicated above. As reported in Molenaar and Campbell (2009), none of the 22 individuals had factor solutions that corresponded to the Big 5.

This example demonstrates how the number of factors determined in a group-level *R-technique* factor analysis may be inconsistent with subsequent individual factor models obtained via individually applied *P-technique* analyses. This is an example of configural invariance; since different persons have different numbers of factors, the pattern of free and fixed factor loadings may be different between persons.[6] Although this difference in number of factors may appear at first to be a quantitative difference, it could also be a qualitative difference between persons since different numbers of factors will result in different configurations and patterns of factor loadings.

CONCLUSION

Very important differences can exist between group-based models that describe heterogeneity in individuals and models that are genuinely person-specific. As we have shown, these models can be distinguished by considering how the individual differences are determined: whether the parameters of a model are estimated based on the group or whether a separate model for each individual is used. This is tied directly to the question of what constitutes a subgroup. For the group-based models, a subgroup represents a prior assignment to a group based on some known variable or, in the case of latent class or mixture models, a certain similarity based on predicted individual characteristics resulting from a group-based common model. In the true person-specific model, separate optimal models are first estimated for each individual. Membership in a subgroup is then determined by identifying those individuals who can be shown empirically to have identical or very similar model structures and then model parameter values. While both modeling approaches can provide useful information, the group-based model comes with one important assumption: namely, that the same model holds for all members of the sample.

For many studies the number of occasions of data that can be collected is limited by the requirements of the design, the burden on study participants, or by the complexity or expense of he data collection procedures. For these situations, the hypothesis represented by the ergodicity assumption, namely, that group models adequately describe individual participants, can only remain untested. For many studies, especially those made possible through intensive data methods based on experience sampling methodology or ecological momentary assessment (Trull & Ebner-Priemer, 2009) operating using devices such as *smartphones* to provide intensive time-series data, sufficient data to test the ergodicity assumption and, if necessary, estimate individual person-specific models becomes a possibility. For studies including videorecording coding of events can also provide sufficient time-series data for estimating person-specific models. Observing mothers with their infants receiving an inoculation, Rovine, Sinclair, and Stifter (2010) estimated individual models using a hidden Markov model. Teti, Mayer, Kim, and Countermine (2010) collected intensive data using a number of different methods (e.g., videorecording, actigraph, self-reported diaries) to provide person-specific data looking at the quality and patterns of infant sleep behaviors and parents' responses to those behaviors. These are only a couple of examples of the many possibilities now available as it becomes simpler to collect more intensive data.

This really only represents the tip of the iceberg in terms of person-specific methods that researchers should learn about. These methods include dynamic factor analysis (Molenaar, 1985; Wood & Brown, 1994), state-space modeling (Molenaar, 2003), control modeling (Simon, 2006), and a host of other methods developed to respond to questions and problems in engineering, econometrics, and the social sciences.

Although these methods are not necessarily appropriate or relevant for all studies, given the possible violation of the *ergodicity* assumption, researchers should consider whether a person-specific component would fit into their research agenda.

NOTES

1. We note the common usage in the literature describing the process of fitting data using a straight line (intercept and slope) or a higher-order polynomial as a "growth" curve model. The term is often whether the process being modeled is growth or change.

2. The term, longitudinal factor analysis, can have many different meanings. In this chapter, we will typically use it to refer to a factor analysis based on relatively few occasions.

3. From this point when we use the term correlation, it will be implicit that the association coefficient could be a correlation, covariance, or sum of the cross-products depending on the requirements of scaling for the model.

4. We also indicate the observed variables as squares. In many SEM programs, regression relationships among latent variables (often shown as circles) are modeled. For observed variable regression, latent variables are set as equivalent to observed variables.

5. There is a set of techniques known as three-mode factor analysis (Bentler & Lee, 1978), which makes use of all three dimensions of the data box.

6. Differences could also result from differences in factor correlations (closer to one for one person; somewhat smaller resulting in two factors for a second person).

REFERENCES

Bath, K. E., Daly, D. L., & Nesselroade, J. R. (1976). Replicability of factors derived from individual p-technique analyses. *Multivariate Behavioral Research*, 1(2), 147–156.

Bentler, P. M., & Lee, S. Y. (1978). Statistical aspects of a three-mode factor analysis model. *Psychometrika*, **43**, 343–352.

Birkhoff, G. (1931). Proof of the ergodic theorem. *Proceedings of the National Academy of Sciences of the United States of America*, **17**, 656–660.

Borkenau, P., & Ostendorf, F. (1998). The big five as states: How useful is the five-factor model to describe intraindividual variations over time? *Journal of Research in Personality*, **32**, 202–221.

Bryk, A., & Raudenbush, S. (1992). *Hierarchical linear models: Applications and data analysis methods*. Newbury Park, CA: Sage Publications.

Cattell, R. B. (1966). The data box: Its ordering of total resources in terms of possible relational systems. In R. B. Cattell (Ed.), *Handbook of multivariate experimental psychology* (pp. 67–128). Chicago, IL: Rand-McNally.

Corneal, C. C. (1990). Stepdaughters' experience of the stepdaughter/stepfather relationship: An investigation of emotional response patterns. Unpublished doctoral dissertation. Penn State University: University Park, PA.

Corneal, S. E., & Nesselroade, J. R. (1991). Multivariate, replicated, single-subject, repeated measures design: Studying change in the adolescent. In R. Lerner, A. Petersen, & J. Brooks-Gunn (Eds.), *Encyclopedia of adolescence* (pp. 681–687). New York, NY: Garland.

Goldstein, H. (1995). *Multilevel statistical models* (2nd ed.). (London, England: Edward Arnold and New York, NY: Halsted.

Gorsuch, R. L. (1983). *Factor analysis* (2nd ed.). Hillsdale, NJ: Erlbaum.

Harman, H. (1976). *Modern factor analysis* (3rd ed., Revised). Chicago, IL: University Chicago Press.

Henderson, C. R. (1975). Best linear unbiased estimation and prediction under a selection model. *Biometrics*, **31**, 423–447.

Joreskog, K. G., & Sorbom, D. (1996). *LISREL8:User's reference guide*. Chicago, IL: Scientific Software International.

Kenny, D. A. (2005). *Cross-lagged panel design. Encyclopedia of statistics in behavioral science*. New York, NY: Wiley.

Laird, N. M., & Ware, J. H. (1982). Random-effects models for longitudinal data. *Biometrics*, **38**(4), 963–974.

Lamiell, J. T. (1981). Toward and idiothetic psychology of personality. *The American Psychologist*, **36**, 276–289.

Liu, S., Rovine, M. J., & Molenaar, P. C. (2012). Selecting a linear model for longitudinal data: Repeated measures analysis of variance, covariance pattern models and growth curve approaches. *Psychological Methods*, **17**(1), 15–30.

Lutkepohl, H. (2006). *New introduction to multiple time series analysis.* New York, NY: Springer.

McArdle, J. J., & Epstein, D. (1987). Latent growth curves within developmental structural equation models. *Child Development,* **58,** 110–133.

Mitteness, L. S., & Nesselroade, J. R. (1987). Attachment in adulthood: Longitudinal investigation of mother-daughter affective interdependencies by p-technique factor analysis. *The Southern Psychologist,* **3,** 37–44.

Molenaar, P. C. M. (1985). A dynamic factor model for the analysis of multivariate time series. *Psychometrika,* **50,** 181–202.

Molenaar, P. C. M. (2003). *State space techniques in structural equation modeling: Transformation of latent variables in and out of latent variable models.* University Park: The Pennsylvania State University.

Molenaar, P. C. M. (2004). A manifesto on psychology as idiographic science: Bringing the person back into scientific psychology, this time forever. *Measurement,* **2,** 201–218.

Molenaar, P. C. M., & Campbell, C. G. (2009). The new person-specific paradigm in psychology. *Current Directions in Psychological Science,* **18**(2), 112–117.

Muthén, B., & Shedden, K. (1999). Finite mixture modeling with mixture outcomes using the EM algorithm. *Biometrics,* **55**(2), 463–469.

Nagin, D. S. (1999). Analyzing developmental trajectories: A semiparametric group-based approach. *Psychological Methods,* **4,** 139–157.

Nesselroade, J. R., & Molenaar, P. C. M. (1999). Pooling lagged covariance structures based on short, multivariate time series for dynamic factor analysis. In R. H. Hoyle (Ed.), *Statistical strategies for small sample research* (pp. 223–250). Thousand Oaks, CA: Sage Publications.

Raiche, G., Riopel, M., & Blais, J.-G. (2006). *Non graphical solutions for the Cattell's scree test.* Paper presented at the International Annual meeting of the Psychometric Society, Montreal.

Robinson, G. K. (1991). The BLUP is a good thing: The estimation of random effects. *Statistical Science,* **6**(1), 15–32.

Rovine, M. J., Molenaar, P. C. M., & Corneal, S. E. (1999). Analysis of emotional response patterns for adolescent stepsons using P-technique factor analysis. In R. K. Silbereisen & A. von Eye (Eds.), *Growing up in times of social change* (pp. 261–285). Berlin, Germany: De Gruyter.

Rovine, M. J., & Molenaar, P. C. M. (2000). A structural modeling approach to the random coefficients model. *Multivariate Behavioral Research,* **35**(1), 51–88.

Rovine, M. J., Sinclair, K. O., & Stifter, C. A. (2010). Modeling mother-infant interactions using hidden Markov models. In K. Newell & P. C. M. Molenaar (Eds.), *Individual pathways of change in learning and development* (pp. 51–67), Washington, DC: APA Press.

Simon, D. (2006). *Optimal state estimation.* New York, NY: Wiley-Interscience.

Sterba, S. K., & Bauer, D. J. (2010). Matching method with theory in person-oriented developmental psychopathology research. *Development and Psychopathology,* **22,** 239–254.

Stone, R. (1947). On the interdependence of blocks of transactions. *Journal of the Royal Statistical Society B,* **9,** 1–32.

Teti, D. M., Mayer, G. E., Kim, B.-R., & Countermine, M. (2010). Maternal emotional availability at bedtime predicts infant sleep quality. *Journal of Family Psychology,* **24**(3), 307–315.

Trull, T. J., & Ebner-Priemer, U. W. (2009). Using experience sampling methods/ecological momentary assessment (ESM/EMA) in clinical assessment and clinical research: Introduction to the special section. *Psychological Assessment,* **21**(4), 457–462.

Walls, T. A., & Schafer, J. L. (2006). *Models for intensive longitudinal data.* New York, NY: Oxford University Press.

Wood, P., & Brown, D. (1994). The study of intraindividual differences by means of dynamic factor models: Rationale, implementation, and interpretation. *Psychological Bulletin,* **116,** 166–186.

Wright, S. (1934). The method of path coefficients. *Annals of Mathematical Statistics,* **5,** 161–215.

Zevon, M. A., & Tellegen, A. (1982). The structure of mood change: An idiographic/nomothetic analysis. *Journal of Personality and Social Psychology,* **43,** 111–122.

VII. REPLICATION, RESEARCH ACCUMULATION, AND META-ANALYSIS IN DEVELOPMENTAL SCIENCE

Noel A. Card

This article is part of the issue "Developmental Methodology" Card (Issue Author). For a full listing of articles in this issue, see: http://onlinelibrary.wiley.com/doi/10.1111/mono.v82.2/issuetoc.

The progression of scientific knowledge requires replication of research results and an orderly accumulation of research knowledge. However, developmental science, like many other sciences, has too often prioritized individual studies at the expense of replication and synthesis efforts. In this chapter, I describe the concepts of replication and research accumulation and consider both their barriers and potentials for developmental science. I emphasize the importance of considering effect sizes rather than statistical significance, and I describe meta-analysis as a powerful tool in facilitating research accumulation and in guiding replication efforts. By considering advancement in terms of research accumulation rather than single studies, developmental science can achieve greater efficiency and precision to guide both future research and applied efforts.

An empirical approach to advancing understanding of human development requires three critical topics that are the focus of this article. First, empirical results should be replicable, and the process of replication advances our understanding. Second, the orderly progression and accumulation of empirical results should produce a more complete understanding of human

Corresponding author: Noel A. Card, University of Connecticut, Storrs, CT; email: noel.card@uconn.edu
DOI: 10.1111/mono.12301

development. Third, meta-analysis is a valuable methodological tool with which to draw conclusions from the accumulation of research results.

Despite the value of replication and the accumulation of empirical knowledge, developmental science—like many other sciences—has not prioritized these efforts. In this chapter, I encourage both individual scientists and developmental science as a field to place greater emphasis on replication, research accumulation, and synthesis through meta-analysis, and I offer recommendations for conducting this work. In the first section of this article, I will focus on replication, describing the importance but also the challenges of replication work, and offer recommendations for how we might conduct replications in developmental science. In the second section, I will describe a model of research accumulation that includes both novel and replication studies that collectively lead to greater understanding of human development. In the third section, I will briefly describe meta-analysis as a tool for quantitatively synthesizing programmatic lines of research. In the fourth and final section, I will describe the opportunities of a developmental science in which replication, research accumulation, and meta-analysis are emphasized, and I will offer recommendations for how we might reach these opportunities.

REPLICATION

An empirical approach to understanding human development relies upon observable study results. In turn, the observable study results should be reproducible across occasions and scientists. This ideal of reproducibility motivates efforts at replication, or conducting a study identical or similar to a previous study to assess whether the same or similar results are obtained. When a study is conducted that follows the procedures of a prior study as closely as possible, this is termed an "exact replication" (Keppel, 1982; another commonly used term is "direct replication" by Schmidt, 2009). A study that is conducted using similar methodology as a prior study but with one or more methodological details altered (e.g., using a different measurement instrument, sampling a different age) is termed an "inexact replication" (Keppel, 1982; also termed "conceptual replication" by Schmidt, 2009).

The Need for Replication

As mentioned, replications represent a fundamental aspect of empirical science. Nevertheless, replication studies seem to be rare in many fields. A survey of 100 psychology journals estimated that just over 1% of published studies were replications (Makel, Plucker, & Hegarty, 2012). A recent survey of two developmental journals suggests a similarly low rate of replication in developmental science (Duncan, Engel, Claessens, & Dowsett, 2013). There have been several recent calls urging more replication in various fields, such as a 126-page special section of *Perspectives on Psychological Science* published by the Association for Psychological Science (see Pashler & Wagenmakers, 2012). The widespread neglect of replication efforts suggests systemic challenges that exist across disciplines.

One reason for the need for greater efforts toward replication comes from our reliance on Null Hypothesis Significance Testing (NHST) and the view that statistically significant results are informative, whereas the absence of statistically significant results is uninformative. From this perspective, there is a danger of publication bias, in which studies with statistically significant results are more likely to be published and those without statistically significant results are likely to go unpublished in scientists' file drawers (Rosenthal, 1979). In addition to publication biases, scientists may engage in questionable research practices (John, Loewenstein, & Prelac, 2012; Simmons, Nelson, & Simonsohn, 2011) such as selectively reporting significant effects (e.g., one measure of the construct "worked" while the others was viewed as problematic), reanalyzing data with various subsets of participants (e.g., removing some children from the analysis; analyzing results separately by gender without a priori expectation), giving extra scrutiny to analysis results that are "almost" statistically significant, or performing a large number of analyses with some subsequently being presented as hypothesized (i.e., HARKing, or Hypothesizing After Results are Known; Kerr, 1998). I do not mean to imply that most developmental scientists intentionally misrepresent data, and I suspect that such instances are rare. But when scientists work in an environment in which data analyses are complex, studies are conducted by multiple individuals, and research reports involve an often long, ongoing process through the iterative peer review process, such biases in reporting results could emerge.

The threat of biases in results reporting or publication likelihood means that the collection of reported results in the published research literature might not accurately represent the results of all studies conducted. In the worst case, it might be that our developmental journals are filled with the 1 out of 20 study results that are statistically significant simply by chance (i.e., the commonly followed Type I error rate of .05). Ioannidis (2005), a medical researcher, published an influential article titled "Why Most Published Research Findings Are False." Given the possibility that many—or even some—of the published research results appearing in developmental journals might be inaccurate, there is a clear need to evaluate study findings through replication studies.

The Barriers to Replication

Despite the need for more replication studies, there are a number of barriers to these efforts. There are several barriers to more widespread efforts to replicate. Journals (i.e., reviewers and editors) often place greater emphasis on novelty than replication (Nosek, Spies, & Motyl, 2012). One reason for this is that journals compete for citations, and the first articles to establish a phenomenon may be more often cited than subsequent replications. Grant funding often goes to novel research proposals, so as universities and other institutions emphasize grant-funded research, researchers will be incentivized to produce novel research, and in turn disincentivized from replication. Some have suggested special journals for replication studies, but these have so far not been widely adapted, and may suffer from poorer reputations than other journals (Giner-Sorolla, 2012). Others have suggested a model in which students engage in replication studies in order to learn the methodologies of an area (e.g., Frank & Saxe, 2012; Grahe et al., 2012); however, this is likely not practical outside of simple studies and is likely impossible for longitudinal studies that comprise much of developmental research (see Card & Little, 2007). The practice of encouraging replications efforts primarily by students may also stigmatize replication studies as something performed only by students (i.e., as something a more established, knowledgeable scientist would not perform). These barriers represent formidable challenges that would be difficult to overcome as individual scientists; instead, it is necessary that disciplines as a whole take steps to promote replication efforts.

A Critique of Replication Literature

The literature on replication has been extremely valuable in pointing to the tremendous need for replication studies and suggesting potential solutions. However, I view two major limitations to much of this literature. First, most of this literature approaches the issue from a Null Hypothesis Significance Testing (NHST) framework (e.g., Ioannidis, 2005). Within this framework, study results are described in terms of significance versus nonsignificance and replications studies can either replicate (i.e., make the same conclusion of significance/nonsignificance) or fail to replicate (i.e., make a different conclusion of significance/nonsignificance) the original study. The NHST framework is problematic in failing to emphasize that all inferential conclusions are probabilistic and in failing to consider the magnitudes of effects. A second limitation of much of the replication literature is that it is written from fields that emphasize experiments and deemphasize individual differences. I argue that developmental science, while certainly using experimental designs, has achieved greater balance than many other fields in focusing on the person, context, and developmental timing variations in effects (versus simply focusing on singular effects). For this reason, as I describe later, it is likely that the majority of studies in developmental science can be thought of as inexact rather than exact replications.

RESEARCH ACCUMULATION

To counter the two critiques I have made toward much of the replication research, I next present an alternative approach based on research accumulation. The key components of this approach include (a) replications focused on effect sizes and (b) a programmatic line of research involving both exact and inexact replications.

Replications Focused on Effect Sizes

As mentioned, replication efforts are commonly framed within an NHST framework, in which a second study either replicates or fails to replicate the original research result. To illustrate the substantial shortcomings of this framework for replication, consider two scenarios. In Scenario 1, the first study of 50 families identifies a positive correlation between a parenting behavior and a child outcome, $r = 0.33$, $p < .05$. The second replication study also samples 50 families, finding $r = 0.27$, ns (here, $p = .058$, which might be acknowledged as "close" to significance). In this scenario, a strict adherence to NHST would suggest a failure to replicate, and even a less strict following would likely conclude ambiguity in the findings. Consider a second scenario: In Scenario 2, the first study is a large study of 1,000 schoolchildren. This study finds a positive correlation between some aspect of peer relations and school performance, $r = 0.70$, $p < .05$. The second replication study also examines 1,000 schoolchildren, finding $r = 0.10$, $p < .05$. In this second scenario we have clear evidence of replication, if our focus is only on significance versus nonsignificance.

The conclusions of replication based on the NHST framework in these two scenarios are extremely problematic. In the first scenario, Study 1 found a significant correlation, whereas Study 2 failed to replicate this finding. Comparisons of the correlations, which index the effect sizes, within these studies show that the two studies found very similar results: $rs = 0.33$ and 0.27. A strict following of significance decisions without considering effect sizes leads to ambiguity about the overall results, and misses the high similarity in results across these two studies. In Scenario 2, the NHST framework leads to the conclusion that the result was replicated (which is true only in the sense that both studies concluded that the association was not zero), but misses the wide difference in effect sizes ($rs = 0.70$ and 0.10) found in these two studies.

Although the effect sizes and sample sizes of these two scenarios were selected to illustrate these points, they are not necessarily unrealistic. There are two key points that I hope these examples illustrate. First, a reliance on the dichotomous significance/nonsignificance decisions of NHST has the potential to overstate small differences in the results of two studies simply because they may straddle two sides of the arbitrary Type I error line (commonly .05). Second, the failure to directly compare effect sizes may

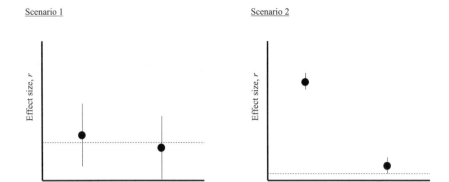

FIGURE 1.—Two hypothetical scenarios of a replication effort.

obscure meaningful differences in study results that would be valuable to understand. A focus on effect sizes and confidence intervals in replication studies overcomes these limitations. Figure 1 shows the effects sizes (correlation coefficients, r) for the two hypothetical scenarios described above. On the left is Scenario 1, in which the two studies fall on opposite sides of the critical value for statistical significance (dashed line, critical $r = 0.28$ in this example), but have similar effect sizes and highly overlapping 95% confidence intervals around their point estimates of the effect sizes. On the right is Scenario 2, in which two studies fall on the same side of the critical value for concluding statistical significance (here, critical $r = .06$ due to large sample size), but have clearly different effect sizes and nonoverlapping confidence intervals around those point estimates of the effect sizes. Figure 1 makes clear that, from the perspective of effect sizes, Scenario 1 is an instance of clear replication, whereas Scenario 2 is an instance of nonreplication. Note that this conclusion about replication based on effect sizes contradicts the conclusions about replication from an NHST perspective.

Rosenthal (1991) has suggested that most variables in the social sciences likely have some association, so it is important to understand the magnitudes and not merely the presence of effects. If this is true, then replication efforts focusing on effect sizes are more valuable than the more common focus on statistical significance conclusions. At the same time, the very concept of replication, even if based on effect size, contains limitations. First, it is important to remember that the probability of a replication falling within the confidence interval of the original study is lower than many people expect. For example, the probability of a replication study falling within the 95% interval of the original study is only 0.83 (assuming normal distributions, a single population standard deviation, and equal sample sizes across studies; see Cumming & Maillardet, 2006; Estes, 1997). The reason for this is that both studies represent imprecise estimates of the population effect size, so there are two sources of imprecision. Second, and more fundamentally, the question of replication itself focuses on single studies, leaving questions of which of the two studies provides the best estimate of effect size regardless of whether replication is considered successful or not. To overcome this latter challenge, I argue that developmental science should shift toward an emphasis on programmatic lines of research.

Programmatic Lines of Replication Research

Earlier, I reviewed the reasons why replications studies are needed. Indeed, the quality of knowledge in developmental science will improve as we conduct individual studies that attempt to replicate prior studies. However, I argue that developmental science can best advance by attending to a programmatic line of multiple studies, rather than focusing on individual studies. The value of any single replication study lies less in whether it supports or refutes—or, following the arguments of the previous section, provides similar or discrepant effects size estimates. Instead, the value of each replication effort lies in providing an accumulation of knowledge about effect sizes of interest. A shift toward this approach to understanding would deemphasize the importance of the results of single studies and place greater emphasis on the collective results of all relevant studies. In practice this shift is already occurring: as an increasing number of developmental scientists conduct increasing numbers of studies, the amount of empirical information should necessitate this shift of attention from individual studies to collections of research evidence. Therefore, this suggested approach simply explicates a trend that is already occurring. As I elaborate next, this shift toward programmatic lines of research would value both exact and inexact replications.

The value of a series of studies that are exact replications of one another rests in the increasing precision of point estimates of a common effect size. The hypothetical Scenario 1 that I described earlier can illustrate this process. Returning to Figure 1, we see that Study 1 provided a point estimate of $r = 0.33$, but it had a large 95% confidence interval, ranging from a lower bound $r = .06$ to an upper bound $r = 0.56$. In other words, the state of knowledge after Study 1 would be that the parenting behaviors studied are positively related to child outcomes (i.e., the result was statistically significant according to conventional criteria), but the magnitude of this association could be small, medium, or large (according to Cohen's guidelines of 0.1, 0.3., and 0.5 for interpreting correlations). This imprecision in knowledge is rather unsatisfying from a scientific view, and likely useless in terms of making recommendations for practice or policy.

The addition of Study 2 in this hypothetical scenario, in addition to serving as a replication for the first study, is valuable in providing more precise knowledge. Combining the results of Study 1 ($r = 0.33$, 95% CI = .06 to 0.56) and Study 2 ($r = 0.27$, 95% CI = −.01 to 0.51) results in an improved estimation of the effect size with more precision than is provided by either study individually. Here, (fixed-effects) meta-analytic combination of the results of these two studies yields an average $r = 0.30$ with a 95% confidence interval ranging from 0.11 to 0.47. In this example, the addition of a second study improves the precision of the estimated effect size a modest amount.

From the traditional perspective of replication, these two studies might be considered sufficient: Study 1 found an effect and Study 2 replicated this effect. However, from the perspective of research accumulation, the more meaningful question is whether there is value in conducting additional exact replications to obtain a more precise estimate to this association. In other words, is a 95% confidence interval of $0.11 < r < 0.47$ sufficient, or is there value in seeking a more precise estimate? If there is value in greater precision, then additional exact replication studies are worthwhile. To extend this hypothetical illustration, we might imagine that four additional studies are conducted: Study 3 ($N = 50$, $r = 0.35$), Study 4 ($N = 50$, $r = 0.25$), Study 5 ($N = 50$, $r = 0.26$), and Study 6 ($N = 50$, $r = 0.34$). The combination of these four studies provides a 95% confidence interval of $r = 0.19$ to 0.40. By following this programmatic line of exact replication studies, the field has progressed by improving the precision of our estimate of this effect size. This tendency is shown in Panel A of Figure 2: As more exact replications of an effect are conducted, our understanding of the magnitude of an effect becomes increasingly precise.

In the proposed approach to research accumulation, there is also value in inexact replications. In fact, outside of tightly controlled studies using homogeneous samples (or studying an effect that does not vary across populations sampled), most replications are probably closer to inexact replications than exact replications: Differences in sampling procedures, selection of measures, and procedures could very likely lead to differences in results in most domains of developmental science. In the proposed model of research accumulation, inexact replications—whether the methodological differences from prior studies are unintentional or deliberate—have value in advancing out understanding.

Consider first the situation in which replication attempts are unintentionally inexact replications; that is, the methodological differences between studies are unplanned. In this situation, it is useful to borrow from the conceptualization of random effects models from meta-analysis (see e.g., Chapter 10 in Card, 2012). Rather than conceptualizing a single effect size that each study is intended to estimate (i.e., a fixed effect), we can think of the population-level effect sizes as having a distribution based on the numerous potential methodological differences between studies. Therefore, the effect size of every study will be centered around some overall population average (the typical effect size from all the studies that could be done), will deviate from this population average based on unknown methodological features of

A) Exact replications

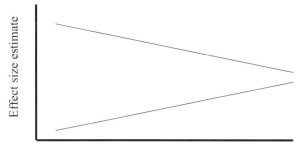

B) Unplanned inexact replications

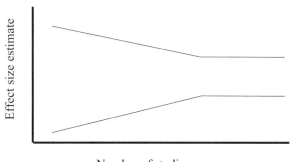

C) Planned inexact replications

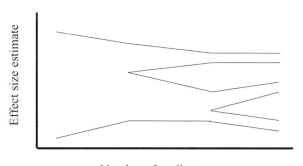

FIGURE 2.—Three patterns of programmatic lines of research.

this type of study (i.e., population-level variance in effect sizes), and will further deviate from the population value for this type of study due to sampling fluctuation. The implication of this population-level variability in effect sizes due to unintended (and unknown) methodological differences across studies is that there will be limits to the precision with which the effect size can be estimated. In the situation described earlier, in which every study is an exact replication of previous studies (i.e., a fixed-effect effect size), each additional study will result in a narrower confidence interval of the overall effect size (Panel A in Figure 2). In the situation in which every study is an inexact replication with unplanned methodological differences, there will be a limit to the precision of estimating effect sizes. This latter tendency is shown in Panel B of Figure 2, in which the precision of estimating an effect size increases initially, but reaches a point where the population-level variability precludes further increases in precision.

A third method of research accumulation would involve inexact replications with deliberate (i.e., planned) deviations in methodology from prior studies. For instance, a developmental researcher might intentionally sample a different age, sample from a different setting, use a different measure, or otherwise deliberately vary the methodology from prior studies. As shown in Panel C of Figure 2, these types of planned inexact replications can, if the methodological feature varied impacts effect sizes, result in a more refined understanding of effects. In this scenario, our overall conclusions become nuanced, of the form "the effect sizes ranges from 0.20 to 0.30 for this group (or this measure, etc.) and ranges from 0.50 to 0.60 for this group (measure, etc.)." This nuanced information is necessary to describe complex systems of person, context, and development.

In each of the three situations described here (a series of exact replications, a series of unplanned inexact replications, and a series of planned inexact replications), the additional studies provide value beyond mere replication of the results of the original study. From this framework of research accumulation, our knowledge of human development rests upon the entire collection of research results, rather than on single studies.

META-ANALYSIS

From the perspective of basing our knowledge on collections of research results rather than individual studies, one of the most valuable endeavors is the systematic review, specifically meta-analyses. Here, I briefly describe systematic reviews and meta-analysis in particular. I then describe the advantages and challenges to using meta-analysis techniques in synthesizing programmatic lines of research in developmental science.

114

Overview of Meta-Analysis

Meta-analysis is a series of techniques for synthesizing programmatic lines of empirical research results. Here, I provide only a brief overview of the techniques of meta-analysis (for fuller coverage see Card, 2012; Cooper, Hedges, & Valentine, 2009; Lipsey & Wilson, 2001; Rosenthal, 1991). Meta-analyses can be considered in terms of five general steps (Cooper, 2009).

The first step is to identify a topic or research questions. Meta-analyses usually have an explicit set of inclusion/exclusion criteria to define the type of studies to include. Clear explication of these criteria defines the population of studies considered (i.e., the programmatic line of research described above). These criteria also reduce potential biases in decisions about whether studies should be included (e.g., without such criteria, a review might give greater scrutiny toward excluding a study with results that contradicts expectations). At this first step, meta-analysts also articulate research questions for the review. Importantly, these research questions are framed in terms of effect size, so that the answers obtained from meta-analyses inform the magnitude as well as statistical significance of effects.

The second step is to search for the literature. Meta-analyses typically use search strategies that are far more exhaustive than typical reviews (e.g., forward and backward searches, searches of multiple disciplinary databases). The exhaustive nature of these searches maximizes the amount of information (i.e., number of studies) from which conclusions are drawn, and may also reduce biases if a nonrepresentative sample was considered. The search strategies used in meta-analyses are commonly reported in publications of meta-analyses, so the searches are potentially replicable; this may also reduce biases in decisions to exclude studies. Importantly, most meta-analyses seek to obtain both published and unpublished study results. Thus, meta-analyses can evaluate the presence of publication bias, and are certainly less susceptible to these biases than traditional literature reviews.

The third step in meta-analysis is to code studies. One aspect of this coding is to extract study results in the form of effect sizes. These effect sizes quantify the direction and magnitudes of study results in a metric that can be combined and compared across studies. In most meta-analysis, this step also involves coding study features such as sample characteristics, measures, and procedures. These coded study features are useful both in describing the existing literature in a field as well as for comparing different types of studies, as described further below.

The fourth step is the actual data analysis. Although the details of this step are beyond the scope of this article, I briefly describe general approaches below. Here, I simply note that the conclusions reached within meta-analytic reviews are based on statistical principles. Although there are potential differences of opinions about the best methods of analysis in meta-analyses, it might be hoped that there is less subjectivity in the conclusions than in other types of literature reviews. In one study, Cooper and Rosenthal (1980) compared the conclusions reached from two groups of students evaluating a collection of research reports; students in the group trained to use meta-analytic techniques reached more comparable conclusions, whereas students in the group using traditional review techniques varied more in their conclusions. Moreover, those using traditional review techniques perceived the research findings as more inconsistent and smaller in magnitude than those using meta-analytic techniques (perhaps in part to the problems of drawing conclusions from statistical significance that I described above). In short, the data-analytic techniques of meta-analysis represent an established and powerful means of drawing conclusions from existing research results.

The fifth step is to present the results of the meta-analysis. It is worth noting that a presentation that both summarizes what is known from the existing research and offers suggestions for further studies is likely to be especially valuable.

Synthesis of Programmatic Lines of Research

As mentioned, I do not describe the statistical details of meta-analysis techniques here. Instead, I simply describe an overview of these techniques as they relate to my previous argument for developmental scientists to focus on programmatic lines of research rather than individual studies. The simplest type of meta-analysis is a fixed-effects analysis of average effect sizes. Here, one assumes that there is a single population effect size, and each study effect size deviates from that population effect size by sampling fluctuation alone. Fixed-effects meta-analyses synthesize effect sizes by using weighted averages, in which studies that provide more precise estimates of effect sizes (due in large part to sample size) are weighted more than studies providing less precise estimates. If we synthesize programmatic lines of developmental research from using fixed-effects meta-analyses, then the value of each additional study lies in providing a more precise estimate of this single population effect size. This situation is directly associated with Pattern A in Figure 2, in which each study is an exact replication of previous studies.

The key assumption of fixed-effects meta-analyses is of homogeneity, that the studies differ from a single population effect size by sampling fluctuation alone. Although this assumption of homogeneity might exist in tightly controlled experiments with homogeneous samples, I believe that this assumption is typically unrealistic for most meaningful effects influenced by individual differences, context, and developmental timing. Fortunately, this assumption of homogeneity is easily tested using meta-analysis techniques. The most common approach to testing this assumption is the Q statistic (Hedges & Olkin, 1985). This test involves summing the weighted squared

116

deviations of study effect sizes from the average effect sizes, and quantifying these deviations as the statistic Q. If Q is statistically significant, then we reject the null hypothesis of homogeneity and accept the alternative hypothesis of heterogeneity. In contrast, if the Q is nonsignificant then we fail to reject the null hypothesis of homogeneity. Like all statistical inferences, this Q test can be underpowered, and therefore, fail to indicate heterogeneity when it exists, and a finding of significant heterogeneity does not imply large or meaningful differences across studies.

In the presence of heterogeneity, it is necessary to meta-analytically combine study results using a random effects model.[1] Random-effects models differ from fixed-effects models in assuming that the population effect sizes consists of a distribution rather than a single point. In other words, random-effects models assume that every study effect size is due to three sources: a population average effect size, population-level deviations from this average (e.g., that a particular study used methodologies that tend to yield higher or lower than average effect sizes), and sampling fluctuation. Meta-analyses based on random-effects models estimate the magnitude of population-level variability in effect sizes (i.e., heterogeneity), and then incorporate these estimates into the precision weighting of the synthesis of effect sizes. This heterogeneity limits the overall precision of effect size estimates; this situation is shown in Panel B of Figure 2. The presence of heterogeneity and the use of random-effects meta-analyses are appropriate when programmatic lines of developmental research consist of inexact replications in which between-study methodological differences are unplanned and/or unknown.

However, methodological differences between inexact replications may be known, either when planning studies (i.e., intentionally sampling a different age range) or through post hoc comparisons of methodologies. Well-conducted meta-analyses typically code various study features such as sample, type, and procedures. These coded study features then can be systematically and quantitatively evaluated as predictors of between-study variability in effect sizes. In other words, meta-analysis techniques allow us to not only model the between-study variability in effect sizes, but to attempt to statistically evaluate whether coded study features are systematically associated with differences in effect sizes obtained in studies. For example, meta-analysis techniques comparable to ANOVA would allow for the comparison of results of studies using one type or measure versus another (e.g., observations versus parent reports of parenting behaviors). Meta-analysis techniques comparable to regression can be used to evaluate continuous variable study features (e.g., average age of samples used in studies), and these regression-based techniques can be used to isolate study features that uniquely predict differences in effect sizes (e.g., separating age versus measurement, which might covary across studies). These meta-analytic comparisons across different types of studies provide the nuanced type of information shown in Panel C of Figure 2. This nuanced information is best derived if the programmatic line of research consists of planned inexact replications, but could also be obtained if the methodological features of inexact replications are identified post hoc (see Lipsey, 2003, for some cautions in interpreting these meta-analytic comparisons).

Although I have provided only a brief overview of meta-analytic techniques, it should be clear that these data analysis tools combined with a developmental science that emphasizes programmatic lines of research offers great opportunities for advancing our understanding in developmental science. Such an approach would not only overcome the challenges of science that are the focus of replication literature, but would serve as readily available repositories of all that is known about a developmental phenomenon. Further, although meta-analyses are commonly performed on a body of previously conducted research, it is possible to perform ongoing meta-analyses (sometimes referred to as "cumulative meta-analyses"). If the ongoing meta-analyses of programmatic lines of research were commonplace in developmental science, they could guide the choices to conduct further studies by suggesting the likely value of either exact replications or various types of inexact replications (including the useful information that particular studies offer little additional value beyond what is currently known). As an increasing number of developmental scientists conduct an increasing number of studies that are published (or not) in an increasing number of developmental journals, it may be that efforts to synthesize research using meta-analytic techniques take on greater importance than adding to a mountain of unsynthesized empirical results with another study.

Although there is clear value in meta-analytic techniques applied to programmatic lines of developmental research, there are still challenges in such an approach. First, the continued reliance on NHST and greater valuation of significant rather than nonsignificant (i.e., noninformative) results will continue to place biasing pressures on what scientists report and publish, which in turn creates a biased state of knowledge no matter how this knowledge is synthesized. Second, meta-analytic techniques are not commonly taught in developmental training programs and are therefore not well understood. Therefore, there are likely misunderstandings about the process of conducting meta-analyses (e.g., the time and resource demands) and the value of meta-analysis results. Third, our science still primarily reinforces, through journal space and grant funding, the individual study. It will take a large shift on our thinking about the advancement of developmental science to begin to deemphasize individual studies and emphasize research accumulation and synthesis. Fourth, meta-analyses can only synthesize the types of studies that exist. For example, in areas of research where most studies focus on interindividual differences, meta-analyses can only synthesize those results but cannot inform intra-individual development.

Thus, new studies using different perspectives (e.g., intraindividual development; see Davis-Kean and Jager, Chapter 3, this volume; Grimm, Davoudzadeh, and Ram, Chapter 4, this volume), new methodologies (e.g., longitudinal as opposed to cross-sectional; see Rush and Hofer, Chapter 5, this volume), and studying different phenomena remain valuable in providing a research basis that could only later be synthesized.

CONCLUSIONS

Given the fundamental premise that empirical results should be reproducible, there is a clear value of replication studies in developmental science. However, as for many other disciplines, there are clear challenges for replication studies in developmental science. A key challenge is that top journals and granting agencies may prioritize novelty over replication. Developmental science will benefit from developing ways to promote replication efforts.

In this chapter, I have argued that the literature on replication has too often been framed in terms of NHST. Adapting Rosenthal's observation of the social sciences, it seems likely that most aspects of development (whether cognitive, behavioral, or social) change across time and covary with other aspects changing across time. Therefore, there are likely few truly zero effects in developmental science. Instead, our focus should be on the magnitudes (which also subsumes directions) of change and covariation; that is, we should consider research results in terms of effect sizes. From this perspective, the important question of replication is not about reaching the same conclusion of significance versus nonsignificance, but in terms of identifying similar effect sizes across studies.

I also argued that developmental science should look beyond individual replication studies, and instead focus on programmatic lines of developmental research. Such a shift represents more than simply a "forest" over "tree" perspective; but explicitly conveys that understanding comes from the accumulation of results from multiple studies rather than a single study (even if it is our own). A focus on programmatic lines of research is benefited through meta-analysis techniques of identifying, quantifying, and analyzing study features and results. Various analytic approaches would variously allow for increased precision in identifying effect sizes (i.e., fixed-effects meta-analyses), identify the limits in our ability to increase precision through further studies (i.e., random-effects meta-analysis), and provide more nuanced conclusions about how differences in study methodologies (e.g., sample, measures, procedures) relates to differences in study effect sizes. These meta-analytic techniques could be applied both retrospectively to previous studies and prospectively to help guide to conduct of future studies.

The arguments I have presented for increasing attention on replication, programmatic lines of research, and meta-analytic synthesis has several implications for developmental science. First, such efforts would identify the value of both exact and inexact replications efforts, depending on the state of a line of research. In some cases, there is a need for exact replications, and in others, the field would benefit from more efforts at inexact replication to evaluate the limits of a phenomenon. In some cases, another study adds little to our understanding, and such information would be valuable in directing resources toward other efforts. Second, a focus on programmatic lines of research, rather than individual studies, would encourage a more integrative interpretation of research findings across researchers, methodologies, and contexts. Third, the greater use of meta-analysis of existing research seems critical in the current research climate, in which the number of studies conducted and published in most areas outpaces the ability of anyone but the most specialized scholar from understanding these findings. Perhaps meta-analyses represent a more cost-effective and impactful contribution than another primary study in many areas of developmental science.

NOTE

1. Indeed, current best practices are to use random-effects models regardless of the results a the Q test. The reasons for this practice are due both to the limitations of the Q test as a statistical inference and to the fact that random effects models mathematically approach fixed effects models as heterogeneity becomes small. Therefore, there are no disadvantages, and potentially many advantages, to using random-effects models by default.

REFERENCES

Card, N. A. (2012). *Applied meta-analysis for social science research.* New York, NY: Guilford Press.

Card, N. A., & Little, T. D. (2007). Longitudinal modeling of developmental processes. *International Journal of Behavioral Development,* **31**, 297–302.

Cooper, H. M. (2009). *Research synthesis and meta-analysis: A step-by-step approach.* Thousand Oaks, CA: Sage.

Cooper, H., Hedges, L. V., & Valentine, J. C. (Eds.) (2009). *The handbook of research synthesis and meta-analysis* (2nd ed.). New York: Russell Sage Foundation.

Cooper, H., & Rosenthal, R. (1980). Statistical versus traditional procedures for summarizing research findings. *Psychological Bulletin,* **87**, 442–449.

Cumming, G., & Maillardet, R. (2006). Confidence intervals and replication: Where will the next mean fall? *Psychological Methods,* **11**, 217–227.

Duncan, G. J., Engel, M., Claessens, A., & Dowsett, C. J. (2013). *The value of replication for developmental science.* Unpublished manuscript.

Estes, W. K. (1997). On the communication of information by displays of standard errors and confidence intervals. *Psychonomic Bulletin & Review,* **4**, 330–341.

Frank, M. C., & Saxe, R. (2012). Teaching replication. *Perspectives on Psychological Science*, **7**, 600–604.

Giner-Sorolla, R. (2012). Science or art? How aesthetic standards grease the way through the publication bottleneck but undermine science. *Perspectives on Psychological Science*, **7**, 562–571.

Grahe, J. E., Reifman, A., Hermann, A. D., Walker, M., Oleson, K. C., & Nario-Redmond, M., et al. (2012). Harnessing the undiscovered resource of student research projects. *Perspectives on Psychological Science*, **7**, 600–604.

Hedges, L. V., & Olkin, I. (1985). *Statistical methods for meta-analysis*. San Diego, CA: Academic Press.

Ioannidis, J. P. A. (2005). Why most published research findings are false. *PLoS Medicine*, **2**, e124.

John, L. K., Loewenstein, G., & Prelec, D. (2012). Measuring the prevalence of questionable research practices with incentives for truth telling. *Psychological Science*, **23**, 524–532.

Keppel, G. (1982). *Design and analysis: A researcher's handbook*. Englewood Cliffs, NJ: Prentice-Hall.

Kerr, N. L. (1998). HARKing: Hypothesizing after the results are known. *Personality and Social Psychology Review*, **2**, 196–217.

Lipsey, M. W. (2003). Those confounded moderators in meta-analysis: Good, bad, and ugly. *The Annals*, **587**, 69–81.

Lipsey, M. W., & Wilson, D. B. (2001). *Practical meta-analysis*. Thousand Oaks, CA: Sage.

Makel, M. C., Plucker, J. A., & Hegarty, B. (2012). Replications in psychology research: How often do they really occur? *Perspectives on Psychological Science*, **7**, 537–542.

Nosek, B. A., Spies, J. R., & Motyl, M. (2012). Scientific utopia: II. Restructuring incentives and practices to promote truth over publishability. *Perspectives on Psychological Science*, **7**, 615–631.

Pashler, H., & Wagenmakers, E.-J. (2012). Editors' introduction to the special section on replicability in psychological science: A crisis of confidence. *Perspectives on Psychological Science*, **7**, 528–530.

Rosenthal, R. (1979). The "file drawer problem" and tolerance for null results. *Psychological Bulletin*, **86**, 638–641.

Rosenthal, R. (1991). *Meta-analytic procedures for social research* (rev. ed.). Newbury Park, CA: Sage.

Schmidt, S. (2009). Shall we really do it again? The powerful concept of replication is neglected in the social sciences. *Review of General Psychology*, **13**, 90–100.

Simmons, J. P., Nelson, L. D., & Simonsohn, U. (2011). False-positive psychology: Undisclosed flexibility in data collection and analysis allows presenting anything as significant. *Psychological Science*, **22**, 1359–1366.

VIII. THE PAST, PRESENT, AND FUTURE OF DEVELOPMENTAL METHODOLOGY

Todd D. Little, Eugene W. Wang, and Britt K. Gorrall

This article is part of the issue "Developmental Methodology" Card (Issue Author). For a full listing of articles in this issue, see: http://onlinelibrary.wiley.com/doi/10.1111/mono.v82.2/issuetoc.

This chapter selectively reviews the evolution of quantitative practices in the field of developmental methodology. The chapter begins with an overview of the past in developmental methodology, discussing the implementation and dissemination of latent variable modeling and, in particular, longitudinal structural equation modeling. It then turns to the present state of developmental methodology, highlighting current methodological advances in the field. Additionally, this section summarizes ample quantitative resources, ranging from key quantitative methods journal articles to the various quantitative methods training programs and institutes. The chapter concludes with the future of developmental methodology and puts forth seven future innovations in the field. The innovations discussed span the topics of measurement, modeling, temporal design, and planned missing data designs. Lastly, the chapter closes with a brief overview of advanced modeling techniques such as continuous time models, state space models, and the application of Bayesian estimation in the field of developmental methodology.

Corresponding author: Todd D. Little, Department of Educational Psychology, Research, Evaluation, Measurement and Statistics (REMS) Concentration, Texas Tech University, PO Box 41071, Lubbock, TX 79409-1071; email: yhat@ttu.edu
Special thanks to Huda Sarraj for assisting in early phases of the development of this Chapter. This work was supported by grant NSF 1053160 (Wei Wu & Todd D. Little, co-PIs) and by the Institute for Measurement, Methodology, Analysis, and Policy at Texas Tech University (Todd D. Little, Director).
DOI: 10.1111/mono.12302

PAST

The logic of latent variables and their mathematical representation has been in the arsenal of developmental methodologists for over a century (e.g., Spearman, 1904). Factor analysis opened up a wealth of methodological opportunities that, over the course of the 20th century, evolved into an exquisite family of statistical tools that are amazingly powerful and flexible (Cudeck & McCallum, 2007). In spite of these statistical advances, however, the broad world of longitudinal structural equation modeling (SEM) is, for the most part, underutilized across the social and behavioral sciences. The widespread adoption of latent variable SEM has been hindered by a number of obstacles including its inherent complexity, computer limitations, software limitations, and curmudgeonly critiques. A core set of developmentalists, on the other hand, have embraced latent variable SEM as the statistical analysis tool of choice. These developmentalists and their like have the training and expertise to effectively shape the tool to properly address the research question at hand.

Unfortunately, because the methodological world is burgeoning with new advances, even methodologically sophisticated developmentalists are hard pressed to take full advantage of the power and flexibility of latent variable SEM. Works such as the current volume and others are essential in order to keep the pipeline of knowledge about developmental methods flowing. By so doing, developmentalists can continue to be leaders in applying the advanced methods to the challenging questions surrounding growth, change, and transformation. These processes are at the core of both developmental theory and developmental methods.

Historically speaking, developmental methods did not emerge as a dedicated topic for developmentalists until after the 3rd edition of the *Handbook of Child Psychology* (Carmichael & Mussen, 1970). Baltes and Nesselroade (1979), both champions of best-practice developmental methods and catalysts of innovation in this area, provided a historical summary of developmental methodology up to the late 1970s. Their overview chapter appeared in their edited volume dedicated to developmental methodology (Nesselroade & Baltes, 1979b). In 1987, the flagship journal of child developmentalists (*Child Development*) published a special issue devoted to methodology (see Connell & Tanaka, 1987). This special issue had a powerful impact on the course of discovery in the field of developmental psychology. These methodological articles have garnered around 2,400 citations as of this writing.

PRESENT

Now, some two score years later, numerous books (e.g., Frees, 2004; Hedeker & Gibbons, 2006; Little, 2013; Singer & Willett, 2003; Taris, 2000) monographs (e.g., this volume; McCartney, Burchinal & Bub, 2006), journals (e.g., *International Journal of Behavioral Development*'s Methods and Measures section, *Multivariate Behavioral Research, Psychological Methods*) and edited volumes/handbooks devoted to developmental methods are perched on the desks of most developmental researchers (e.g., Fitzmaurice, Davidian, Verbeke, & Molenberghs, 2008; Laursen, Little, & Card, 2012; Walls & Schafer, 2006; Teti, 2005). In a similar vein, the inaugural Developmental Methods Conference was held in 2012 and has become a regular biennial conference (held again in 2014, 2016, and expected to continue in even years) and will likely become a staple in the knowledge fodder of the developmental community. In addition, a number of training institutes and workshops are available for researchers. Table 1 provides references to a number of the diverse offerings of advanced statistical training workshops and institutes available. The burgeoning availability and popularity of these resources is a testament to the advanced methodological sophistication that is required to address developmental processes.

This volume represents the latest addition to the wealth of resources. The contributions reflect a representative sample of topics and issues in methods that developmentalists can and should utilize. Grimm et al. (Chapter 4) trace the history of longitudinal analysis models since 1979 when Baltes and Nesselroade summarized the state of analysis techniques for modeling change processes. Grimm et al. (Chapter 4) also provide an excellent summary of the

TABLE 1

ADVANCED STATISTICAL TRAINING WORKSHOPS AND INSTITUTES

Training Program	Website
Todd Little's Stats Camp	www.statscamp.org
Inter-university Consortium for Political and Social Research (ICPSR) Summer Program	www.icpsr.umich.edu/
APA's Advanced Training Institutes (ATI)	www.apa.org/science/resources/ati/
University of Texas Summer Statistics Institute	www.stat.utexas.edu/training/ssi
Muthéns' Mplus Short Courses	www.statmodel.com/courses2.shtml
Data Analysis Training Institute of Connecticut (DATIC)	www.datic.uconn.edu/
Curran-Bauer Analytics Workshops	www.curranbauer.org/
The Methodology Center—Penn State	www.methodology.psu.edu/training
Quebec Inter-University Center for Social Statistics (QICSS)	www.ciqss.umontreal.ca/
Latent Variable Methods Workshop	www.lvmworkshop.org/
Data Matters—Data Science Short Course Series	www.datamatters.org/
Serve Inc.—University of North Carolina Greensboro	www.servecenter.org/

rationales for longitudinal studies. They describe variations in the panel model and the growth curve model, both classes of model focus on homogeneous models for characterizing change in a representative samples of persons. Rovine and Lo (Chapter 6) provide a complimentary focus on heterogeneity among persons (e.g., growth mixture modeling) and on ideographic models of within person change (e.g., dynamic p-technique) models. Rush and Hofer (Chapter 5) discuss a mix of the approaches to disentangle via multilevel modeling the intensive within-person variability and the individual differences between persons. Rush and Hofer (Chapter 5) emphasize important design elements that need to be incorporated in order to optimize the ability to capture change processes. Together these three contributions offer us a rather comprehensive view of the analysis models that can be fit to longitudinal data. Below, we will suggest a couple of other models that are emerging and that can be added to the overall arsenal of developmental methods and, like Rush and Hofer (Chapter 5), we also emphasize a number of design and measurement issues that developmentalists must prioritize (e.g., planned missing data designs).

Davis-Kean and Jager (Chapter 3) discuss the advantages and disadvantages in using large-scale surveys. As they intimate, the archival datasets were not designed with latent variables in mind. Most constructs are represented by only a single item which, unfortunately, disallows content validation, unreliability corrections, and invariance testing, for example. Often, too, the surveys reflect a large array of constructs, but the theoretical integration among the constructs is lacking. Sound tests of theory rely on crafting a testable research question and then choosing and measuring the right constructs—not just a kitchen-sink's worth of constructs. Measured constructs should emanate from the same meta-theoretical model in order to provide strong evidence of the relations among the constructs (Little, 2013). The typical consortium of investigators that design the protocols can suffer from the too-many-cooks-in-the-kitchen phenomenon. The result is a recipe that lacks integration. Another core problem of large-scale longitudinal datasets is the lack of attention to the timing of the assessments. Changes take time to unfold (Gollob & Reichardt, 1987; Selig, Preacher, & Little, 2012). Modeling the change process requires effective timing of the measurements or appropriate incorporation of the lag information into the analysis model (Selig et al., 2012). Annual surveys lack sufficient sensitivity to model change processes. As a replication and validation of primary research, the existing large-scale datasets can be useful. Kean-Davis et al. highlight examples.

Jager et al. (Chapter 2) address issues of sampling and generalizability. In particular, they discuss the pros and cons of probability sampling versus the ubiquitous convenience sample. These authors, however, make a compelling argument for homogeneous convenience sampling. Here, restricting the sample to a highly circumscribed population (e.g., sample only from a single ethnic group) would have the advantage of increasing generalizability to the circumscribed population. Quota homogeneous sampling can be used when between-group comparisons of two or more circumscribed populations are evaluated. Given the expense of primary research, incorporating such sampling restrictions has both economic and scientific merit. We suggest coupling this approach with the admonitions of Davis-Kean and Jager (Chapter 3), who encourage us to evaluate the broader generalizability of any findings by validating the findings in the context of large-scale representative samples.

Moving forward, however, greater attention to both design and measurement would greatly increase the scientific value of large-scale data collection projects. Incorporating a unified theoretical model in the design of a protocol provides the necessary cohesion among the constructs to allow strong tests of theory. Using planned missing data designs, for example, is a critical design feature that would increase the value of large-scale data collections. The multi-form protocol, for example, would allow greater coverage of the constructs and can be used to estimate and adjust for test-retest effects, for example (Jorgensen et al., 2014). A wave missing design can be used to more effectively sample the timing of the measurements (Graham, Hofer, & MacKinnon, 1996; Mistler & Enders, 2013; Rhemtulla, Jia, Wu, & Little, 2014). In addition, the two-method planned missing data design can be incorporated to allow anchoring of key constructs with expensive gold-standard assessments (Garnier-Villarreal, Rhemtulla, & Little, 2014). We provide greater details on these designs below. Our point here is that planned missing data design are sorely underutilized in large-scale data collection efforts (see Little, Jorgenson, Lang, & Moore, 2013; Little, Lang, Wu, & Rhemtulla, 2016; Little & Rhemtulla, 2013).

FUTURE

Although developmental methods have come a long way in the last few decades, a number of areas of methodological research are ripe for future innovations. We highlight seven areas of future innovation that we think will guide developmental research in the years to come. The future of developmental methodology is exciting. Developmentalists have a massive array of measurement, design, and analysis advances to utilize. Most of these advances are already available and now they need to be embraced and readily adopted.

Measurement, Measurement, Measurement

The days of using Likert scales to capture responses to questionnaire items should be bygone days. Touch screen technology, GPS tracking capabilities, and computer-assisted audio are just a few of the already available technologies that developmental methodologists should exploit. Researchers would benefit from using truly continuous number lines as response scales, for example. The lost art of measurement is lamentable in that the field has seen very little innovation in the area of measurement. Encouraging students to think about measurement as an important aspect of methodological innovation and creativity is not the norm in graduate training. For example, creatively developing multiple indicators of latent constructs is often beyond the ken of students and faculty alike. Developing multiple indicators is an essential modern measurement issue; yet teaching how to do it is not emphasized or sufficiently taught during the course of quantitative training. Sometimes the solution to creating multiple indicators is rather simple. For instance, a video-taped lesson can be divided into three segments and each segment would receive its own scoring rubric or three trained raters can each rate the video. A standardized test such as the RAVEN progressive matrices can be divided into thirds and ordered by item difficulty—then each form can be administered under a time constraint, yielding three indicators of intellective capability.

When many items or segments of a construct are available, parceling techniques are particularly useful in generating multiple indicators of constructs that possess highly advantageous psychometric characteristic (Bandalos & Finney, 2001). A parcel is an indicator for a latent construct that is comprised of the average of to two or more items. The many merits as well as the mathematics of parcels have been well documented (Little, Cunningham, Shahar, & Widaman, 2002; Little, Rhemtulla, Gibson, & Schoemann, 2013). Although some authors still have well-warranted cautions to consider in the use of parceling (Bandalos & Finney, 2001; Marsh, Lüdtke, Nagengast, Morin, & Von Davier, 2013; Sterba & MacCallum, 2010), the thoughtful and careful use of parcels has attendant benefits that outweigh the potential missteps that might occur when they are improperly deployed.

A related issue on this theme of measurement and tradecraft is how new scales should be developed. Contrary to popular mantra, the use of exploratory factor analysis (EFA) for developing a scale is at best misguided and at worst misguiding. Scale development is a theory-driven enterprise and should be analyzed using a theory-guided analysis tool, namely, confirmatory factor analysis (CFA; Brown, 2012). EFA is a data-driven enterprise that presents too many misguiding temptations for misunderstanding the nature of the construct of interest. Using CFA with careful and skillful scrutiny of all indicated modifications will reveal the structure of a scale that will retain optimal validity. A related note on the test-development methods of yore, and especially from the perspective of developmental methodology, using the outmoded method of test-retest reliability is nearly apocryphal to creating measures that are sensitive to the goal of modeling change unless the retest interval is massively shorter than the expected developmental change interval.

Modeling, Modeling, Modeling

The advances in modeling techniques coincide with evolving philosophical viewpoints on scientific epistemology (Rodgers, 2010). We argue that optimal scientific progress is made by adopting a pragmatic modeling perspective where a priori and a posteriori decisions about modeling data are applied in a thoughtful and balanced manner. This modeling perspective involves having an engaged dialog with data to thoroughly reconcile the meaningful model modifications against the various and spurious sources of sampling and parsimony error. Researchers should be empowered to navigate, with scientific acumen, the path along the model-data trail. The emphasis in this dialog is honing and pruning models to optimize the model-driven test against data. Then statistically principled choices among models yields a final rendering that is presented to the field. The informed field can then scrutinize the presented model's adequacy. As Rodgers (2010, p. 10) describes this shift in methodological perspective, "Engaging in science as a creative process requires thinking scientifically in creative ways . . .. Building and evaluating statistical and mathematical models encourages creativity."

At the heart of creativity in modeling is the skill and expertise that are normally associated with words such as craft, dexterity, and artistry. The rule-bound mechanistic methods that have typified the scientific research process have lost their ability to manage the complexity of modern modeling. The scope of contemporary theorizing and the concomitant statistical applications needed to test the adequacy and verisimilitude of a model requires flexible and principled application of the techniques of the trade. Such tradecraft is born of training but also experience. Working with master craft colleagues to establish partnerships or research teams is, as we mentioned above, a future feature of how developmental work will need to be conducted. Creating such teams and organizing internal checks and balances can also provide important safeguards against conflicts of interested and unethical conduct when high-stakes can occlude wise judgment.

Design, Design, Design

We highlight a number of design innovations that should become a matter of course when it comes to conducting developmental research. The traditions of the field are still vestiges of ANOVA design restrictions. With modern estimation capabilities and modern modeling machinery, the innovations in design can now be accommodated rather easily at the analysis phase. Of course, theory and unequivocally articulated research questions must precede and guide these design considerations.

128

Planned Missing Data Designs

Planned missing data designs should become the norm for designing developmental studies. Modern missing data treatments (e.g., Full Information Maximum Likelihood [FIML] estimation or Multiple Imputation [MI]; see Enders, 2010; Graham, 2012; Van Buuren, 2012) are very powerful and, because of software efficiencies as well as hardware computational capabilities, they are quick and easy to implement. Without going into too much detail, planned missing data satisfy the most lenient of missing data assumptions; namely, that the missing data are missing completely at random (MCAR). When missing data satisfy the MCAR assumption, there is no bias introduced. The existing data look just like what the data would have looked like had there been no missing data. The only loss when the absent data are MCAR is the diminished power that occurs. One very positive feature of modern missing data treatments is that they all provide an estimation mechanism to bring back much of the lost power.

Planned missing data are, by definition, MCAR because the absent data were randomly controlled by the experimenter. Assuming the random assignment procedure was truly random then the data have no associations with any aspect of the study design or the extant data. Since the power loss is remediated with modern treatments there is very little that can undermine the validity of the conclusions when planned missing designs are employed. In fact, planned missing data designs carry a number of features that provide added benefits over a traditional complete case study. These benefits include reducing the amount of unplanned (and potentially biasing) missing data, reducing the burden (on both experimenter and participant) during the whole data collection process, minimizing the effects of fatigue on the response effort of the participants, reducing test reactivity, minimizing, and allowing the estimation of retest effects, reducing study costs, and what not. These attendant benefits of planned missing data design are sorely underappreciated and woefully underutilized.

Three broad classes of planned missing data design are available for use. The first design is the multiform design of which the three-form planned missing data design is the easiest and most straightforward to implement (Graham et al., 1996). This design involves assigning all items in a protocol to one of four blocks of items that are labeled X, A, B, and C. Here, the number of items in each block does not need to be equal. The X block contains items that all participants see (e.g., demographic items, single-item constructs, critical grouping variables, and the like). The remaining items are assigned to the A, B, and C block in such a way that the between-block canonical correlation is maximized. Then three forms are created by combining the four blocks: (1) X + A + B, (2) X + A + C, and (3) X + B + C. Participants are then randomly assigned to receive one of the three forms; thereby insuring the missing items are MCAR. In terms of sample size considerations, Jia et al. (2014), suggest a minimum of 120 persons. Jorgensen et al. (2014) offer suggestions for how to assign the multiform protocols across waves of a given study and, through the use of a clever design feature, they also demonstrate how to effectively estimate and control for retest effects across multiple waves.

The second planned missing data design that is underutilized is the two-method design. Often developmental researchers have a gold standard measure of behavior or cognition but it is expensive. Often a cheaper measure of the same construct is available but it has bias. In this situation researchers will choose the expensive measure but suffer from being underpowered or choose the biased measure and suffer the bias. The two-method planned missing data design allows the best of both worlds. By using a bifactor latent variable approach both measures of the same construct are given and allowed to load on the common construct factor. A bias factor is introduced and only the biased measure is allowed to load on it and the bias is thereby removed. The planned missing part comes in because only about 1/3 of the sample needs to receive the expensive measure in order to estimate the common construct for all participants. Garnier-Villarreal et al. (2014) showed that when the bias factor is unchanging over time, the expensive measure only needs to be administered at two time points. If the bias factor changes over time, the expensive measure needs to be administered at each time point.

Lastly, wave missing designs can be introduced that allow researchers to randomly assign which participants get tested at which time point. Rhemtulla et al. (2014) introduce a way to optimize the efficiency of latent growth parameter when a wave missing design is used. Wu, Jia, Rhemtulla, and Little (2016) follow up with a general procedure to determine the optimal wave missing design depending on the analysis model that will be employed.

A couple of important points need to be made about using planned missing data designs. First, unplanned missing data can still occur (and should still be minimized to the extent possible) and variables that predict the potential unplanned missing data should be included in the study protocol. Second, power and relative efficiency need to be addressed carefully. In this regard, Schoemann, Miller, Pornprasertmanit, and Wu (2014) provide a detailed discussion of how to use Monte Carlo Simulation software to estimate the power of various planned missing data design. Finally, each of the designs can be combined into a given study and any of the features of these designs can be introduced into an ongoing study that had not yet considered using planned missing designs.

Temporal Design

Change takes time to unfold. Causal effects also take time to unfold. To be able to understand such effects we need to be able to model the unfolding process. Sampling time, much as we would sample persons or variables, allows us untapped opportunities to model changes in the magnitude of an effect as the change process or causal effect is unveiled over time. Temporal design is a break from the traditional discrete interval methods that have dominated developmental science. Historically speaking, the limiting factor was that the analysis systems available to researchers required balanced data. R.Q Bell introduced the accelerated longitudinal design in the 1950s and Warner Shaie presented his General Developmental Model for how to design and analyze longitudinal data. These designs and analysis methods were predicated on the limits of repeated measures analysis of variance techniques and the least-squares estimator. Statistical software programs such as R (R Core Team, 2015) have facilitated the implementation of temporal designs in social science research. R adequately handles longitudinal data, efficiently deals with missing data, and the open-source nature of R allows for an expedited roll-out of specialized modeling procedures. Moving social science researchers from point and click analytic programs to programs like R, which are user-driven, enables researchers to become more informed of their statistical analyses and to not be bound by preset specifications in the software. Furthermore, with the advent of estimation methods that can readily handle missing data (MI, FIML, and Bayesian), various features of temporal design can now be exploited. For example, the missing data associated with an accelerated longitudinal design pose no threat to the ability to model age-related changes devoid of cohort and time-of-measurement effects. When properly treated, the missing data reflect the missing at random assumption and, when properly estimated, the effects of cohort differences and time-of-measurement influences can be estimated and, thereby, controlled.

INNOVATIONS IN MODELING

The static panel models that have characterized longitudinal research are moving in directions that have great promise and utility. Two related strands of methodological research are in the areas of continuous time models and state-space models.

Continuous Time Models

To begin the discussion of continuous time models, the first consideration is how change is conceptualized. Conceptualizing change through the lens of discrete time models is limited in its approaches: interactions between measurement occasions are considered nonexistent, they have difficulty handling unequally spaced observations, and, as

131

mentioned above, the results are dependent upon the sampling rate of the data (Deboeck, 2013). Often our research questions are interested in how a variable is changing over time. With continuous time modeling, we can rely on the mathematical simplicity of derivatives to capture a change process. Traditional panel models do not use modeling techniques that adequately represent a variable changing with respect to time. To properly address questions related to such change, systems need to be considered dynamically. In this regard, using derivatives allows for variables to be described as changing with respect to time (Deboeck, 2013).

The language of derivatives is foreign to many researchers in the social and behavioral science fields, however, the language is actually ideal for the social sciences since derivatives measure the rate of change, particularly over time (Deboeck, Nicholson, Bergeman, & Preacher, 2013). The zeroth derivative is a point in time or a score on a particular variable. The first derivative is the slope, the rate at which one variable is change with respect to another (here, time is the other variable). The second derivative is the rate of change of the slope (i.e., how fast the first derivative is changing with respect to time). To assist with understanding of derivatives, consider this example: a car is driving down a freeway, the position of the car at any particular point in time would be the zeroth derivative, the speed in which the car is traveling down the road would be the first derivative, and the acceleration or deceleration of the car, when it occurs, is the second derivative.

Modeling techniques such as differential equation modeling utilize derivative estimates to analyze change with respect to time. Differential equation models express the relationships between the states of variables, and how variables are changing (Brown, 2007; Deboeck et al., 2013). Ferrer, Steele, and Hsieh (2012) and Ferrer, Nesselroade, and Steele (2013) use differential equations to model dyadic interactions. Dynamic factor analysis (DFA) and multilevel modeling (MLM) are currently being used to model dyadic interactions. DFA, however, is challenged to model change in means over time, and MLM cannot characterize intraindividual changes (Ferrer et al., 2012). Differential equation modeling allows researchers to direct their focus on variability to specific time scales, compared to Latent Growth Modeling (LGM) which is concerned with variability over the entire time-span. Deboeck et al. (2013) notes the key difference between Latent Differential Equation modeling (LDE) and LGM is the timescale in which the two models are applied, with LDE using an embedding matrix to reorganize the data where each row consists of a subset of the extended time series.

In this discussion of continuous time models and how to measure change, attention must be directed to intraindividual variability. Intraindividual variability is typically examined by calculating the within-person standard deviation or coefficient of variation (CV) of a person's time series (Deboeck,

Montpetit, Bergeman, & Boker, 2009). These approaches are incomplete and limited because the ordering of observations and sampling rate (times at which measurements are collected) are often not taken into consideration. The uses of derivatives to calculate change are not hindered by the limitations of the coefficient of variation or the intraindividual standard deviation (Deboeck, Nicholson, Kouros, Little, & Garber, 2015). Generalized Local Linear Approximation (GLLA; Boker, Deboeck, Edler, & Keel, 2009) can be used to examine derivative estimates in a time series, and multiple time series to be examined versus a single time scale. Additionally, GLLA can use any number of observations for derivative estimation, which allows for different time scales to be smoothed over.

As mentioned, discrete time models are dependent on the sampling interval, and this limitation can make it difficult to make comparisons between studies that have different sampling rates. Voelkle and Oud (2013) show that structural equation modeling has the ability to handle irregularly spaced assessment waves, and continuous time models can account for individually varying time intervals. Continuous time modeling by means of structural equation modeling can be summarized in five steps (see Oud & Delsing, 2010; Voelkle & Oud., 2013). Voelkle, Oud, Davidov, and Schmidt (2012) address the problem of time being considered implicitly in such models as auto-regressive and crossed-lagged models. Stochastic differential equations have the ability to explicitly model discrete-time data with the underlying continuous model. Voelkle et al. (2012) presents a stochastic differential equation model in the framework of a structural equation model to aid comprehension.

State-Space Modeling

The collection of intensive repeated measures or time series data (e.g., daily diary designs) has become more prevalent in the social and behavioral sciences (Mehl & Conner, 2013; Walls, 2013; Walls & Schafer, 2006). Intensive repeated measures data are appealing to researchers in the social and behavioral sciences because in addition to the between-person differences being examined, the within-person dynamics and interactions between- and within-person factors can be analyzed as well. The data structure of intensive repeated measures study designs can be problematic: there are large number of measurement occasions, the number of time points can be greater than the number of participants, the data often are not aligned in time for each individual, and large amounts of missing data can occur. Modeling techniques such as Hierarchical Linear Modeling (HLM), Latent Growth Modeling (LGM,) and variants of Structural Equation Modeling (SEM) are not adequately able to model intensive repeated measures data. For example, with SEM and LGM, as the number of measurement occasions (t) surpasses the number of participants (n), estimation issues become increasingly problematic (Chow, Ho, Hamaker, & Dolan, 2010; Gu & Yung, 2013).

State space modeling (SSM) can sufficiently model intensive repeated measures data without suffering the drawbacks that stem from the nature of the data structure. SSM is relatively unknown topic in the social and behavioral sciences, but is strongly rooted within control engineering and econometric disciplines (Commandeur, Koopman, & Oom, 2011). Indeed, Commandeur and Koopman (2007) identify the primary objective of this technique as modeling the dynamic evolutions of observations repeated over time. SSM utilizes observations at one point in time (prior or current) to make predictions about the properties of an unobserved future state. There are a number of advantages to using SSM: missing observations are handled efficiently, estimation procedures are not disrupted, and multiple exogenous and endogenous variables can easily be added into relevant equations (Durbin & Koopman 2001; Gu & Yung, 2013). The state-space model is comprised of two equations: the measurement equation and the transition equation. The measurement equation distinguishes the relationship between the unobserved state vector with a vector of observations, while the transition equation depicts the dynamics of the state through the transition matrix (Song & Ferrer, 2009). The transition matrix reflects the effect that the current state vector has on a predicted future state vector. The state space modeling framework has been expanded to have applications in mediation analysis (Gu, Preacher, & Ferrer, 2014), multilevel regression models, and multilevel confirmatory factor models (Gu, Preacher, Wu, & Yung, 2014).

Bayesian Methods

Bayesian techniques offer exciting opportunities for longitudinal analyses. Bayesian techniques are opening vistas in four (interrelated) areas of analysis: redressing missing data, handling categorical data, small level-2 sample size problems, and heretofore difficult (if not intractable) situations such as cross-classified data (Kaplan, 2014). Bayesian techniques offer improved computational/estimation methods for these situations in which maximum likelihood (ML) has difficulty, even though the estimation methods are asymptotically equivalent (Asparouhov & Muthén, 2010) . In addition, we will propose that Bayesian methods offer theoretical advantages for longitudinal data analysis.

For many years Bayesian methods (i.e., Markov Chain Monte Carlo or MCMC) methods have been one of the top methods for multiple imputation of missing data. Also, in the presence of missing data Bayesian estimation offers a valuable alternative to the weighted least squares (WLS) estimator, because WLS is biased when missing data are missing at random (MAR).

When dependent variables are categorical (nominal or polytomous), ML methods can become unfeasible when the number of latent variables is large because of problems with numerical integration. Bayesian estimation does not suffer from the same limitations. Bayesian estimation can be used to overcome sample size shortcomings of ML estimation (Gelman, Carlin, Stern & Rubin, 2004; Kaplan, 2014; McGrayne, 2011). For example, when the number of level-2 clusters is less than 50, Bayesian estimation can be used to obtain better estimates and more accurate confidence intervals than ML. Longitudinal designs that have cross-classified units (i.e., students who frequently move from classroom to classroom or campus to campus) is not feasible under ML, particularly when the number of level-2 units is small, but these kinds of analyses are feasible using Bayesian estimation, particularly in software packages such as xxM (Mehta, 2013).

Most arguments between frequentists and Bayesians have centered around the use of "non-informative" priors. Longitudinal data analysis, on the other hand, is the perfect setting for using "informative" priors. Here, the wealth of information from prior studies and prior assessment occasions can be leveraged to place tighter intervals on expected values of nearly all model parameters. That is, Bayesian analyses are focused more on the overall distributions (both prior and posterior) of the parameters of a model rather than on point estimates or even confidence intervals. Further, Bayesian methods make no assumptions about the distributional shape of the posterior distribution, and in fact, are ideally suited for dealing with nonnormal distributions. Clearly, many of the new methodological advances in longitudinal data analysis will take advantage of Bayesian methods and thinking. In fact, many applications of ML estimation of confirmatory models are already Bayesian in spirit if not in kind. In this regard, the barriers that have traditionally separated Bayesian from frequentist are permeable and slowly dissolving.

CONCLUSIONS

The future of developmental methods is certainly exciting and filled with both opportunity for discovery and challenges for further methodological development. The epistemological tango between theory and methods has brought us to a near crescendo of possibilities for discovery and advances. The future directions of developmental methods are, in many ways, at the trailblazing frontier of the social and behavioral sciences (and educational, economic, biomedical, and so on). As our discipline embraces these advances and the advances yet to come, the impact of our science will also continue to grow. Being at the frontier of developmental methodology is not only good science, it is a matter of social justice. Bad research informs bad policy and blunts the precision of theory, while good research informs good policy and hones the precision of theory. Doing science well and then making the results approachable is the quintessential goal; in so doing, practitioners, stakeholders, and policymakers can easily resonate with and thereby use the findings from good developmental methodology.

REFERENCES

Asparouhov, T. & Muthen, B. (2010, September 29). Bayesian analysis of latent variable models using Mplus. Version 4. Retrieved from www.statmodel.com

Baltes, P. B., & Nesselroade, J. R. (1979). History and rationale of longitudinal research. In J. R. Nesselroade & P. B. Baltes (Eds.), *Longitudinal research in the study of behavior and development* (pp. 1–39). New York, NY: Academic Press.

Bandalos, D. L., & Finney, S. J. (2001). Item parceling issues in structural equation modeling. In G. A. Marcoulides & R. E. Schumacher (Eds.), *New developments and techniques in structural equation modeling* (pp. 269–296). Hillsdale, NJ: Erlbaum.

Boker, S. M., Deboeck, P. R., Edler, C., & Keel, P. K. (2009). Generalized local linear approximation of derivatives from time series. In S.-M. Chow & E. Ferrar (Eds.), *Statistical methods for modeling human dynamics: An interdisciplinary dialogue.* Boca Raton, FL: Taylor & Francis.

Brown, C. (2007). *Differential equations: A modeling approach.* Thousand Oaks, CA: Sage Publications.

Brown, T. A. (2012). *Confirmatory factor analysis for applied research.* New York, NY: Guilford Press.

Carmichael, L., & Mussen, P. H. (1970). *Carmichael's manual of child psychology.* New York, NY: Wiley.

Chow, S.-M, Ho, M.-H.-R., Hanmaker, E. L., & Dolan, C. V. (2010). Equivalence and differences between structural equation modeling and state-space modeling techniques. *Structural Equation Modeling, 17,* 303–332.

Commandeur, J. J. F, & Koopman, S. J. (2007). *An introduction to state space time series analysis.* New York, NY: Oxford University Press.

Commandeur, J. J. F, Koopman, S. J., & Ooms, M. (2011). Statistical software for state space methods. *Journal of Statistical Software, 41*(1), 1–18. Retrieved from http://www.jstatsoft.org/v4/il/

Connell, J. P., & Tanaka, J. S. (1987). Introduction to the special section on structural equation modeling. *Child Development, 58,* 2–3.

Cudeck, R. C., & McCallum, R. C. (Eds.) (2007). *Factor analysis at 100: Historical developments and future directions.* Mahwah, NJ: Erlbaum.

Deboeck, P. R. (2013). Dynamical systems and models of continuous time. *The Oxford handbook of quantitative methods in psychology (Vol. 2): Statistical analysis,* (pp. 411–431). New York, NY: Oxford University Press.

Deboeck, P. R., Montpetit, M. A., Bergeman, C. S., & Boker, S. M. (2009). Describing intraindividual variability at multiple time scales using derivative estimates. *Psychological Methods, 14,* 367–386.

Deboeck, P. R., Nicholson, J. S., Bergeman, C. S., & Preacher, K. J. (2013). From modeling long-term growth to short-term fluctuations: Differential equation modeling is the language of change. In R. E. Millsap, L. A. van der Ark, D. M. Bolt, & C. M. Woods (Eds.), *New developments in quantitative psychology* (Vol. 66). New York, NY: Springer.

Deboeck, P. R., Nicholson, J. S., Kouros, C. D., Little, T. D., & Garber, J. (2015). Integrating developmental theory and methodology: Using derivatives to articulate change theories, models, and inferences. *Applied Developmental Science*, **19**, 217–231.

Durbin, J., & Koopman, S. J. (2001). *Time series analysis by state space methods*. New York, NY: Oxford University Press.

Enders, C. K. (2010). *Applied missing data analysis*. New York, NY: Guilford Press.

Ferrer, E., Nesselroade, J. R., & Steele, J. S. (2013). An idiographic approach to estimating models of dyadic interactions with differential equations. *Psychometrika*, **79**, 675–700.

Ferrer, E., Steele, J. S., & Hsieh, F. (2012). Analyzing the dynamics of affective dyadic interactions using patterns of intra- and interindividual variability. *Multivariate Behavioral Research*, **47**, 136–171.

Fitzmaurice, G., Davidian, M., Verbeke, G., & Molenberghs, G. (Eds.) (2008). *Longitudinal data analysis: A handbook of modern statistical methods*. London: Chapman & Hall/CRC Press.

Frees, E. W. (2004). *Longitudinal and panel data: Analysis and applications in the social sciences*. New York, NY: Cambridge University Press.

Garnier-Villarreal, M., Rhemtulla, M., & Little, T. D. (2014). Two-method planned missing designs for longitudinal research. *International Journal of Behavioral Development*, **38**, 411–422.

Gelman, A., Carlin, J. B., Stern, H. S., & Rubin, D. B. (2004). Bayesian data analysis (2nd ed.). NY, New York: Chapman & Hall/CRC.

Gollob, H. F., & Reichardt, C. S. (1987). Taking account of time lags in causal models. *Child Development: Special Section on Structural Equation Modeling*, **58**, 80–92.

Graham, J. W. (2012). *Missing data: Analysis and design*. New York, NY: Springer.

Graham, J. W., Hofer, S. M., & MacKinnon, D. P. (1996). Maximizing the usefulness of data obtained with planned missing value patterns: An application of maximum likelihood procedures. *Multivariate Behavioral Research*, **31**, 197–218.

Gu, F., Preacher, K. J., & Ferrer, E. (2014). A state space modeling approach to mediation analysis. *Journal of Educational and Behavioral Statistics*, **39**, 117–143.

Gu, F., Preacher, K. J., Wu, W., & Yung, Y.-F. (2014). A computationally efficient state space approach to estimating multilevel regression models and multilevel confirmatory factor models. *Multivariate Behavioral Research*, **49**, 119–129.

Gu, F., & Yung, Y.-F. (2013). A SAS/IML program using the Kalman filter for estimating state space model. *Behavior Research Methods*, **45**, 38–53.

Hedeker, D., & Gibbons, R. D. (2006). *Longitudinal data analysis*. New York, NY: Wiley.

Jia, F., Moore, E. W. G., Kinai, R., Crowe, K. S., Schoemann, A. M., & Little, T. D. (2014). Planned missing data design on small sample size: How small is too small? *International Journal of Behavior Development*, **38**, 435–452.

Jorgensen, T. D., Rhemtulla, M., Schoemann, A. M., McPherson, B., Wu, W., & Little T. D. (2014). Optimal assignment methods in the three-form planned missing design. *International Journal of Behavioral Development*, **38**, 397–410.

Kaplan, D. (2014), *Bayesian statistics for the social sciences*. New York, NY: Guilford Press.

Laursen, B., Little, T. D., & Card, N. A. (Eds.) (2012). *Handbook of developmental research methods*. New York, NY: Guilford Press.

Little, T. D. (2013). *Longitudinal structural equation modeling*. New York, NY: Guilford Press.

Little, T. D., Cunningham, W. A., Shahar, G., & Widaman, K. F. (2002). To parcel or not to parcel: Exploring the question, weighing the merits. *Structural Equation Modeling*, **9**, 151–173.

Little, T. D., Jorgensen, T. D., Lang, K. M., & Moore, E. W. G. (2013). On the joys of missing data. *Journal of Pediatric Psychology*, **39**, 151–162.

Little, T. D., Lang, K. M., Wu, W., & Rhemtulla, M. (2016). Missing data. In D. Cicchetti (Ed.), *Developmental psychopathology*. (3rd ed., pp. 760–796). New York, NY: Wiley.

Little, T. D., & Rhemtulla, M. (2013). Planned missing data designs for developmental researchers. *Child Development Perspectives*, **7**, 199–204.

Little, T. D., Rhemtulla, M., Gibson, K., & Schoemann, A. M. (2013). Why the items versus parcels controversy needn't be one. *Psychological Methods*, **18**, 285–300.

Marsh, H. W., Lüdtke, O., Nagengast, B., Morin, A. J. S., & Von Davier, M. (2013). Why item parcels are (almost) never appropriate: Two wrongs do not make a right—camouflaging misspecification with item parcels in CFA models. *Psychological Methods*, **18**, 257–284.

McCartney, K., Burchinal, M., & Bub, K. (Eds.) (2006). *Best practices in quantitative methods for developmentalists. Monographs of the Society for Research in Child Development*, Hoboken, NJ: Wiley-Blackwell.

McGrayne, S. B. (2011). *The theory that would not die: How Bayes' rule cracked the Enigma code, hunted down Russian submarines & emerged triumphant from two centuries of controversy.* New Haven, CT: Yale University Press.

Mehl, M. R., & Conner, T. S., (2013). *Handbook of research methods for studying daily life.* New York, NY: Guilford Press.

Mehta, P. (2013) *xxM user's guide.* Houston. TX: University of Houston.

Mistler, S. A., & Enders, C. K. (2013). Planned missing data designs for developmental research. In B. Laursen, T. D. Little, & N. A. Card (Eds.), *Handbook of Developmental Research Methods* (pp. 742–754). New York, NY: Guilford Press.

Nesselroade, J. R., & Baltes, P. B. (Eds.) (1979b). *Longitudinal research in the study of behavior and development.* New York, NY: Academic Press.

Oud, J. H., & Delsing, M. J. (2010). Continuous time modeling of panel data by means of SEM. In K. van Montfort, J. Oud, & A. Satorra (Eds.), *Longitudinal research with latent variables* (pp. 201–244). New York, NY: Springer.

R Core Team. (2015). R: A language and environment for statistical computing. R Foundation for Statistical Computing, Vienna, Austria. URL http://www.R-project.org/

Rhemtulla, M., Jia, F., Wu, W., & Little, T. D. (2014). Planned missing designs to optimize the efficiency of latent growth parameter estimates. *International Journal of Behavior Development*, **38**, 423–434.

Rodgers, J. L. (2010). The epistemology of mathematical and statistical modeling: A quiet methodological revolution. *American Psychologist*, **65**, 1–12.

Schoemann, A. S., Miller, P. J., Pornprasertmanit, S., & Wu, W. (2014). Using Monte Carlo simulations to determine power and sample size for planned missing designs. *International Journal of Behavioral Development*, **38**, 471–479.

Selig, J. P., Preacher, K. J., & Little, T. D. (2012). Modeling time-dependent association in longitudinal data: A lag as moderator approach. *Multivariate Behavioral Research*, **47**, 697–716.

Singer, J. D., & Willett, J. B. (2003) *Applied longitudinal data analysis: Modeling change and event occurrence*, New York, NY: Oxford University Press.

Song, H., & Ferrer, E. (2009). State-space modeling of dynamic psychological processes via the Kalman smoother algorithm: Rationale, finite sample properties, and applications. *Structural Equation Modeling*, **16**, 338–363.

Spearman, C. (1904). "General Intelligence," objectively determined and measured. *The American Journal of Psychology*, **15**, 201–292.

Sterba, S. K., & MacCallum, R. C. (2010). Variability in parameter estimates and model fit across random allocations of items to parcels. *Multivariate Behavioral Research*, **45**, 322–358.

Taris, T. (2000). *Longitudinal data analysis*. Thousands Oak, CA: Sage Publications.

Teti, D. M. (2005). *Handbook of research methods in developmental science*. Oxford: Blackwell Publishing.

Van Buuren, S. (2012). *Flexible imputation of missing data*. Boca Raton, FL: Chapman & Hall/CRC press.

Voelkle, M. C., & Oud, J. H. L. (2013), Continuous time modelling with individually varying time intervals for oscillating and non-oscillating processes. *British Journal of Mathematical and Statistical Psychology*, **66**, 103–126.

Voelkle, M. C., Oud, J. H., Davidov, E., & Schmidt, P. (2012). An SEM approach to continuous time modeling of panel data: Relating authoritarianism and anomia. *Psychological Methods*, **17**, 176–192.

Walls, T. (2013). Intensive longitudinal data. In T. D. Little (Ed.), *Oxford handbook of quantitative methods (Vol 2): Statistical analyses*, (pp. 432–440) New York, NY: Oxford University Press.

Walls, T., & Schafer, J. L., (Eds.) (2006). *Models for intensive longitudinal data*. New York, NY: Oxford University Press.

Wu, W., Jia, F., Rhemtulla, M., & Little, T. D. (2016). Search for efficient designs for analysis of change: A Monte Carlo approach. *International Journal of Behavioral Development*, **48**, 1047–1061.

COMMENTARY

OBSERVATIONS ABOUT HOW WE LEARN ABOUT METHODOLOGY AND STATISTICS

Paul E. Jose

This article is part of the issue "Developmental Methodology" Card (Issue Author). For a full listing of articles in this issue, see: http://onlinelibrary.wiley.com/doi/10.1111/mono.v82.2/issuetoc.

The overarching theme of this monograph is to encourage developmental researchers to acquire cutting-edge and innovative design and statistical methods so that we can improve the studies that we execute on the topic of change. Card, the editor of the monograph, challenges the reader to think about works such as the present one as contributing to the new subdiscipline of developmental methodology within the broader field of developmental science. This thought-provoking stance served as the stimulus for the present commentary, which is a collection of observations on "how we learn about methodology and statistics." The point is made that we often learn critical new information from our colleagues, from seminal writings in the literature, and from conferences and workshop participation. It is encouraged that researchers pursue all three of these pathways as ways to acquire innovative knowledge and techniques. Finally, the role of developmental science societies in supporting the dissemination and uptake of this type of knowledge is discussed.

Corresponding author: Paul E. Jose, Victoria University of Wellington, Wellington, New Zealand, email: paul.jose@vuw.ac.nz
DOI: 10.1111/mono.12303

I have read the contents of this monograph now several times, and I have noticed that many voices are heard in this lengthy monograph (16 authors by my count), so considerable variability in perspectives is evident. But at the same time, I was struck by several important themes that emerged across the various contributions. I will not reiterate the key topics of the entire monograph, as this has been done well by Card in the first chapter. My job, as I see it, is to make observations about the thrust of the entire monograph taken as a whole. What I noticed as a common theme across all of the chapters was a keen desire by all of the writers to impart to the reader important new information about how we should go about the work of exploring change in our research.

As a consumer of written works such as the present monograph, and as an instructor of methodology and statistics, I spend a lot of time thinking about how to maximize our efforts to improve the knowledge and skills of students and colleagues in the area of developmental methodology. The contents of my commentary, then, will not be a recounting of the many important new ways of thinking about designing developmental studies and analyzing data over time—the present monograph stands very well on its own in this regard—rather it will constitute a set of observations about the meta-theme of the present work, namely, are we doing a good job of enabling our students and colleagues to become more adept developmental methodologists?

I admit at the outset that much of this commentary will be written from my first person perspective. I suppose I could dress it up by claiming validity as a "participant informant," but that seems disingenuous even to me. I would like to rely upon an established literature for my observations, but little research has been performed on this topic. I will cite appropriate studies where relevant. Another caveat is that I know that my experiences are not universal. Other people will have had different trajectories through life. Regardless, I think my observations and suggestions will resonate with many readers, and hopefully, as a result, we can take the enterprise of improving developmental methodology instruction more seriously.

The narrative of my commentary will consider several ideas in sequence. I first want to discuss who is likely to read published works such as a Society for Research in Child Development (SRCD) monograph dedicated to developmental methodology. Second, I would like to offer some reflections about using methodology and statistics as a tool to achieve a particular end. Third, I want to entertain the question, "How do most researchers upgrade their knowledge base and skills to keep current in the field?" And fourth and last, I would like to respond to Card's suggestion that we strive to create a subdiscipline within developmental science called "developmental methodology."

WHO READS SUCH A WORK AS THIS, AND WHY?

If you have made it through the introduction to this paragraph to reach this point, I can make an educated guess about your personal characteristics based upon about 35 years as a methodology and statistic instructor who has also written articles on this topic. You are likely to positively value the role of methodology and statistics within the field of developmental psychology (or an allied field focused on the study of change). You are probably motivated to learn new, cutting-edge developments in developmental methodology, and you are keen to apply what you have learned here to improve the quality of your own research in terms of design and data analysis. I would also guess that this volume will be read avidly by master's and PhD students and by young scholars early in their career as they are typically keen to improve their understanding and familiarity with methodology. In other words, for many readers, reading this monograph fulfills a very practical and real world need: namely, to upskill one's ability to conduct sophisticated and sensitive research that will be published in high-impact factor journals. I do not for a moment wish to impugn this pragmatic motive to become a more accomplished researcher. Instead, I want to take some time in this commentary to humanize the research process and try to be self-aware about our goals and motives in what we do. By doing so, I seek to acknowledge some typically unspoken truisms about conducting developmental research.

THE "TOOL" OF DEVELOPMENTAL METHODOLOGY

I confess that sometimes while I am teaching research design and statistics, I fall back on the trope that learning statistics is like learning how to use a tool. A good carpenter, for example, needs to learn how to successfully operate a radial arm saw, and, I argue to my disoriented students, learning how to compute and interpret a repeated measures analysis of variance is a similar achievement in the field of developmental psychology. Some students' expressions suggest that their interest in learning ANOVA is essentially the same as their interest in learning how operate a radial arm saw, namely, not in the least, but a goodly number of students seem to grasp the gist of this imperfect analogy and struggle on. For a few individuals, learning about methodology and statistics is an end in itself, and mastering a complicated type of analysis is a worthy standalone goal. For most researchers, however, knowledge of research designs and statistics is a means to more important goals, that is, finishing one's thesis, obtaining a grant, and/or publishing one's research findings. This motive, unfortunately, sometimes leads students (and even seasoned researchers) to say to instructors of methodology and statistics ill-considered things such as, "Just tell me what to do, and I'll do it . . ."

As Bob Abelson put it in his excellent book, *Statistics as principled argument* (1995):

For years I always responded to students who asked, "Can I do this?" by saying something like, "You can do anything you want, but if you use method M you'll be open to criticism Z. You can argue your case effectively, however, if you use procedure P and are lucky enough to get result R. If you don't get result R, then I'm afraid you'll have to settle for a weaker claim. (p. xii)

I learned basic and advanced statistics from Prof. Abelson many years ago, and in his teachings and writings he spoke critically of the "cookbook" approach to statistics exemplified in the previous quote. In this fashion, some students approach the learning of statistics as "a pinch of probability theory, a dash of marginal probabilities, and a soupçon of least squares regression."

To continue with this comparison, what many of us try to do with the teaching of methodology and statistics is to dig below the surface (as Bob instructed us to do) to explain why we recommend doing P and not M. Learning how to make cuts with the radial arm saw while avoiding severing appendages is just the start. Next the budding woodworker needs to understand the subtleties of using particular blades with particular cutting surfaces to effectively make cuts of the right size, precision, and type. Similarly, in the world of methodology, depending upon the size and the type of one's dataset, one would be advised to try analysis P over analysis M in order to obtain the optimal outcome. Readers of this monograph, for the most part, have progressed beyond the "teach me the basics" stage of learning methodology and statistics, and they (namely, you) want to understand the myriad complexities that apply to designing optimal studies and applying best practice data analytic strategies. This monograph does not disappoint on this count, in my view, and it offers numerous new suggestions, explanations, and descriptions that will prove useful for practicing researchers.

These suggestions should best be understood as "rhetorical devices," as defined by Abelson (1995). In his words, "the purpose of statistics is to organize a useful argument from quantitative evidence, using a form of principled rhetoric" (p. xiii). Merriam-Webster's (2016) second definition of rhetoric is "the art or skill of speaking or writing formally and effectively, especially as a way to persuade or influence people." What Abelson was alleging, I would argue, is that skilled researchers employ the art and skill of conducting and reporting their statistical analyses in such a fashion so as to be convincing in their narrative. For example, most researchers know that analyzing nested data is appropriately analyzed with a multilevel modeling approach. Consequently reviewers, editors, and readers increasingly find the following rhetorical strategy to be unpersuasive and unconvincing: "pupils from 12 schools were combined into a single dataset in which amount of mathematics instruction, which varied from school-to-school, was used to predict individual student achievement scores."

As Abelson emphasized, it is important to bear in mind that these rhetorical devices are based on reasoned *principle*. The accumulated literature on methodology and statistics, substantially buttressed by the present monograph, allows us to make these principled arguments. To pick only one example from the many made in this monograph, Rush and Hofer (Chapter 5) suggested that the study of change can be made more robust and reliable by understanding "the merits of measurement-intensive research designs." A researcher who employs a design in which multiple repeated measurements are made can more successfully optimize assessments of a given construct. In particular, assessments of measurement models can be made more sensitive to change by identifying within-person variance as separate from between-person variance (Chapter 5, Figure 3). This strategy is not accepted practice in the research enterprise yet, but as more researchers become aware of it, try it out, find that it can provide new information, and publish papers involving this new technique, then more uptake will occur and it eventually might become an established rhetorical device that researchers routinely use to buttress their arguments.

THE NEED TO CONTINUE LEARNING NEW DEVELOPMENTS IN THE FIELD OF DEVELOPMENTAL METHODOLOGY

So, clearly, researchers need to engage in a career-long search for powerful methodological and statistical strategies that serve as convincing rhetorical arguments if they want to be successful in making a mark on their discipline. How do most researchers navigate this voyage? It is still the case that most individuals in the field receive the bulk of their intensive, detailed instruction in methodology and statistics while attending graduate school at the beginning of their career. Once graduated, scholars seek to maintain their knowledge base chiefly by: 1) learning new techniques from colleagues within their institution; 2) reading journal articles, chapters, or books devoted to topics of methodology and statistics; and 3) attending workshops at conferences or standalone extension learning institutions. Card, in the first chapter of this monograph, mentioned paths 2 and 3, but I am going to talk about these two in more depth as well as add in a third path. I personally recommend pursuing all three avenues, but each possesses its own shortcomings and virtues.

Learning From One's Colleagues

If you are fortunate enough to have a knowledgeable colleague who is willing to tutor you on a topic, then this can be a beneficial arrangement. As one such "knowledgeable colleague" in my department, I can relate that this arrangement is not always salubrious for the provider of the information. A truism in this dynamic is that when I hear "I have a quick statistics question, it will only take 5 minutes," my eyes immediately start furtively glancing for possible exits because I know from repeated dosages that the ensuing conversation will under no circumstance last for 5 or fewer minutes. I encourage solicitors of this type of knowledge to be respectful and compensate providers in some fashion (i.e., a cup of coffee, money, co-authorship, or at the very least, eternal gratitude).

It is usually the case that the providers of this information lecture on this material at some point in the academic year, and one strategy that I would like to see taken up more frequently is for the solicitors of this knowledge to sit in on the provider's course. A case in point comes from my own history, when, as an associate professor approximately 15 years out of graduate school, I decided that the best way for me to learn structural equation modeling (SEM) was to sit in on a graduate-level course taught by a colleague on this topic (thanks, Fred Bryant). I did most of the homework assignments and attended all of the lectures, and in the end I found that I had learned not only the whys but also the very important hows of SEM. Very importantly, I acquired information on topics that I did not know that I needed to know. A common experience that methods and statistics consultants have is that the questioner is often asking the wrong question because they do not know enough about the topic to ask the right question to solve their problem. In fact, it usually takes me about 5 minutes with a questioner just to get to the point where we both understand the issue at hand well enough so that the questioner can ask a helpful question. So, instead of haranguing my colleague with endless questions about the procedures of SEM, I saved him a considerable amount of time by investing my time to learn the basics of conducting SEM analyses.

Another important insight I had about the process of acquiring new methods and statistical techniques was that the hands-on experience with analyzing data in the lab with the other students was where a considerable amount of the most important learning occurred. Sometimes instructors express surprise to me that their students were not able to perform statistical methods that they had lectured on previously. "I showed them very clearly in lecture how to do this analysis, but inexplicably, some of my students failed that part on their homework" they say, but if we can manage to set aside our defensiveness, I think it would be useful to acknowledge that hands-on experience, particularly in terms of methodology and statistics, is a critical method of learning. It is notable that there is a growing literature on this issue in the teaching of statistics (i.e., Moore, 1997; Smith, 1998; Stohr-Hunt, 1996).

I have also attempted to learn new strategies and techniques through reading journal articles and books (and increasingly engaging with online apps, for example, the R Project (2016)). I have found that the chief advantages are that it can be more time-efficient and less expensive than attending lectures or workshops. However, books and articles lack the interactive quality that is of immense value in learning new perspectives and techniques. What do you do when you receive the disheartening message from your statistics program that the model-fitting algorithm did not converge due to a nonpositive definite matrix? Few statistics books take on such low-level phenomena, but it is exactly the sort of frustrating experience that can be expertly dealt with in a class or workshop.

Card emphasized the important contributions of published resources and dedicated works on developmental methodology, such as the previous SRCD monograph entitled *Best Practices in Quantitative Methods for Developmentalists* written by McCartney, Burchinal, and Bub (2006), and the *Handbook of Developmental Research Methods* edited by Laursen, Little, and Card (2012). I agree that we have seen a significant increase in books, handbooks, edited books, and chapters in books on methodology and statistics over the last 20 years. The Sage series of "little green books," formally known as the Quantitative Applications in the Social Sciences, is famous for extending our knowledge in these domains, and it stands as an impressive resource in this area. Publishers like the American Psychological Association (APA), Lawrence Erlbaum, Guilford Press, and others have sections of their booklist dedicated to methodology and statistics. Increasingly, we are seeing journals like the *Educational Psychologist* (September, 2016) create special issues devoted to methods and statistics. Individual articles promoting a particular new developmental method are increasingly being published, for example, the paper entitled "A gentle introduction to Bayesian analysis: Applications to Developmental Research" published in *Child Development* in 2013 by van der Schoot et al. (2013). In short, the written offerings on developmental methodology and statistics are accumulating at a record pace, and self-instruction through reading has never before been so promising or rewarding.

Here, at the end of this section, I would like to respond to those individuals who glibly offer the advice, "Oh, you can pick up these new techniques by reading articles in which they were used." Unfortunately, the truth of the matter is that many details and complexities of design and data analyses are routinely *not* included in published papers on content issues because some editors believe "including them would take too much precious journal space" or "researchers should already know this." Occasionally journal editors will allow an appendix (either at the end of the published paper or in an online archive) to be included that explains subtle issues in the analyses, but this is not typically done. If our studies are to achieve reproducibility (e.g., Ioannidis, 2005), then I would argue that more information, not just about the research procedures but also about the data analyses, should be included in published reports.

Workshops

At the same time, we have seen a dramatic upsurge of opportunities for face-to-face interactions with knowledgeable instructors of methods and statistics. Students 20 years ago would attend the conferences offered by the APA and the SRCD and hope to find a session or two devoted to improving methodological and statistical rigor. Today, these offerings are plentiful and varied. APA always offers a long list of continuing education workshops at its annual meeting, a good number of which address statistical issues such as psychometrics, use of the R package of statistical modules, and other analytic strategies. SRCD, and its companion organization Society for Research on Adolescence (SRA), routinely offer a number of addresses (invited and otherwise) and workshops that push the envelope in methods and statistics. SRCD launched a special topics conference on developmental methodology in 2012, and it followed this initial offering with another 1 or 2 years later, both of which were well attended and positively received. This year, the same conference was continued under the aegis of the same group of scholars who had organized the first two conferences. SRCD wisely invested in this enterprise to get it launched, and now the conference will stand on its own and develop its own identity. As before, it provided 3 days of intensive immersion in a wide range of topics generally concerned with developmental methodology, and it provided many opportunities for young scholars to present their own work as well as discuss new methodological and statistical areas with seasoned scholars.

Another interesting development is the fact that individuals, companies, and organizations outside of the conferences are now offering intensive workshops, generally ranging in length from 1 day to a week, on topics of interest to researchers who want to improve their knowledge and skills in methodology and statistics. These workshops are standalone in that they are not typically tied to conferences or to courses offered by a university, and they have exploded in number and variety over the last decade. A scholar can invest a few days and some amount of money to become knowledgeable in, for example, meta-analysis, SEM, Bayesian data analysis, the treatment of missing values, mediation and moderation, statistical packages (like Mplus or SAS), or any number of other subjects. The fact that these workshops have become popular, I think, speaks to several new realities in academia. First, the proliferation of new methods (both in design and in statistics) has accelerated from what it used to be. Established scholars used to be able to "coast" through their career based on what they learned in graduate school and what their students could teach them. The current rate of innovation makes one's graduate school curriculum obsolete, or at least ineffective, within a shorter amount of time now. Second, scholars cannot sufficiently benefit from the old ways of upgrading knowledge, that is, asking the expert in one's department or consulting with a statistician. One cannot absorb all that is needed to be known about Mplus, for example, by asking a few questions. And third, hands-on or interactive learning, as noted before, is indispensable in the genuine and deep acquisition of these types of learning.

DO WE NEED A DISTINCT SUBDISCIPLINE WITHIN DEVELOPMENTAL SCIENCE CALLED "DEVELOPMENTAL METHODOLOGY?"

For the most part, provision of resources in developmental methodology has grown organically, in other words, certain scholars have discerned the need for greater availability of instruction and materials on developmental methodology, and then they have accordingly generated journal articles, books, special issues, websites, workshops, and so on, to fill these needs. In this fashion, Card and his colleagues decided to organize an SRCD monograph composed of chapters on cutting-edge topics that were felt to be timely and important. In the first chapter, Card explicitly argued that within the broader field of developmental science we should have a distinct and coherent subdiscipline termed "developmental methodology." And, in fact, he goes so far as to offer a provocative claim that the present monograph as a whole should stand as a "flagpost" for "organizing Developmental Methodology as a subdiscipline within the broader field of developmental science" (p. 8). This bold stand deserves some consideration, in my view, as he is clearly trying to convince us to behave differently than we are currently. In particular, he says that the current monograph, in conjunction with the previous SRCD monograph by McCartney et al. (2006) and other related materials, should "facilitate discussion about the unique opportunities and challenges" (p. 9) and "generate further activity" (p. 10) of using advanced methods within developmental science.

His intent has been fulfilled in that he has gotten me sufficiently interested in this idea so that I have "discussed it" here. So what exactly should be done? Card and his colleagues are not specific in this monograph because it was not intended to be a blueprint for action, nor would I argue that my observations here are necessarily a guideline for what we should do. My observations were intended to be a description of what we are currently doing, and, as such, I think a sense of self-reflection and self-assessment is a good place to start. Most of us work in "the trenches," that is, we meet our classes to teach our material, we perform committee work that is mostly focused on our department's or

148

university's needs, we work to write academic reports and papers, and, in contrast, we spend little time with scholars from our broader subdiscipline (in my case, developmental psychology) trying to enact guidelines and procedures that will benefit it. It is often hard work to extract ourselves from the day-to-day work routine to, first of all, become aware of broader issues, and, second of all, to do something that will help the broader discipline.

Despite the blinders I have on, I occasionally raise my head to think about the broader discipline and all of our roles in it, and this essay is one of these occasions. I will be so bold as to suggest one concrete way that we can advance research methodology, and it is relatively easy: familiarize yourself with the SRCD (2016) strategic goals that are currently being discussed and operationalized within the organization. Card's suggestion that we prioritize developmental methodology within the broader field of developmental science is congruent with several of these goals. The first SRCD goal, which seeks to "advance developmental science" by advancing cutting-edge and integrative developmental science research, depends upon researchers being knowledgeable about and capable with new advancements in methodology and statistics. The document specifically promotes the acquisition of "new technologies and methods," which speaks directly to the issue at hand. In addition, Goal 4, which argues that we need to build capacity in our field, highlights, in my view, the need for comprehensive and intense instruction in methods and statistics during graduate school, but also to continue life-long learning through continuing education efforts.

Other developmental science societies also promote similar goals in their mission statements and strategic goals. We may be reaching critical mass within the field of developmental science that would permit cooperation on a world-wide scale. As a case in point, let me point to the founding of ICDSS (International Consortium of Developmental Science Societies) in 2012 (see Sherrod, 2016). The Secretariat of Anne Petersen, Rainer Silbereisen, and Lonnie Sherrod brought together at that time nine founding societies: Cognitive Development Society, European Association for Developmental Psychology, European Association for Research on Adolescence, International Congress for Infant Studies, International Society for the Study of Behavioral Development, Piaget Society, Society for Research on Child Development, Society for Research on Adolescence, and Society for the Study of Human Development. Two additional societies have been added subsequently: Australasian Human Development Association and Society for the Study of Emerging Adulthood.

With seed funding from SRCD, the group will convene its first consensus conference in the Netherlands (Sherrod, 2016) in early 2017 in order to begin formulating ways that these developmental science–based societies can begin to collaborate on writing and disseminating position papers as well as to identify future tasks that can be tackled by the numerous societies working in concert. One of the goals of ICDSS is to facilitate the sharing of resources such as technical knowledge and expertise held by high-income countries with low-income countries. Going back to my initial question in this commentary, "Who reads works such as the present SRCD monograph?," I can argue that it, unfortunately, will not be much read by scholars in Ghana and Vietnam. We need to do a better job of disseminating high-quality methods and statistics expertise, not just to young scholars in high-income countries like Australia and Great Britain, but to middle- and low-income countries around the world as well. It is not clear at this juncture whether ICDSS will take this task on as one of its key goals, but I would like to suggest that it doing so would further Card's vision of a coherent developmental science organization thinking presciently about how to meet the needs of future generations of developmental scientists. For example, we can more effectively engage in developmental science collaborations across cultural boundaries and languages if we have a common language of methods and statistics.

CONCLUSIONS

A common theme is embodied in this monograph: researchers in developmental science are encouraged to acquire more knowledge and skills in designing and implementing high-quality studies of change, as well as data analytic skills that will enable more illuminating and fair descriptions of what our data have to tell us about the phenomenon in question. Card in particular argues that we should begin to think about developmental methodology as a subdiscipline worthy of investment and consideration on its own. He urges us to "facilitate discussion" and "generate further activity," which I wholly support as well. In good heart, I believe that leaders in developmental science have already started the ball rolling on these activities, and it is compelling to say that the future is bright in this regard.

I would offer that several concrete activities that you, readers of this monograph, can do:

1) support and facilitate efforts by your society to provide enrichment and continuing education in the area of developmental methodology;
2) be an avid reader (and citer) of developmental methodology articles and books;
3) "pay back" to whomever is your main source of methods and statistics advice within your unit by supporting institutional recognition and compensation for this/these individual(s);
4) attend workshops on methods and statistics to the extent that you can afford the time and money, and encourage others to attend as well; and

5) attend the biennial Developmental Methodology conference to provide an outlet for your own expertise, build new areas of expertise, and network with leaders in this community.

Many of us who teach and work in the area of methods and statistics are very excited by the growing recognition and esteem of developmental methodology within the broader reach of developmental science, and although our area is broad, deep, and full of energy, much still remains to be done.

REFERENCES

Abelson, R. P. (1995). *Statistics as principled argument.* Hillsdale, NJ: Erlbaum.

Ioannidis, J. P. A. (2005). Why most published research findings are false. *PLoS Medicine,* **2** (8), e124. https://doi.org/10.1371/journal.pmed.0020124

Laursen, B., Little, T. D., & Card, N. A. (2012). *Handbook of developmental research methods.* New York, NY: Guilford Press.

McCartney, K., Burchinal, M. R., & Bub, K. L. (2006). Best practices in quantitative methods for developmentalists. Introduction to the Monograph. *Monographs of the Society for Research in Child Development,* **71** (3), 1–8.

Merriam-Webster Dictionary. (2016). Definition of "rhetoric." Accessed 08/10/16 from http://www.merriam-webster.com/dictionary/rhetoric

Moore, D. S. (1997). New pedagogy and new content: The case of statistics. *International Statistical Review,* **65**, 123–137. https://doi.org/10.1111/j.1751-5823.1997.tb00390.x

R Project. (2016). *The R Project for Statistical Computing.* Downloaded 17/10/16: https://www.r-project.org/

Sherrod, L. (2016). International Consortium of Developmental Science Societies (ICDSS): 2016 Consensus Conference. *SRCD Developments,* **59** (4), 1–2.

Smith, G. (1998). Learning statistics by doing statistics. *Journal of Statistics Education,* **6** (3), 1–10.

SRCD. (2016). *Strategic goals.* Downloaded 10/15/16: http://srcd.org/about-us/strategic-plan/strategic-goals

Stohr-Hunt, P. M. (1996). An analysis of frequency of hands-on experience and science achievement. *Journal of Research in Science Teaching,* **33** (1), 101–109.

van der Schoot, R., Kaplan, D., Denissen, J., Asendorpf, J. B., Neyer, F. J., & van Aken, M. A. G. (2013). A gentle introduction to Bayesian analysis: Applications to developmental research. *Child Development,* **85** (3), 842–860. https://doi.org/10.1111/cdev.12169

CONTRIBUTORS

This article is part of the issue "Developmental Methodology" Card (Issue Author). For a full listing of articles in this issue, see: http:// onlinelibrary.wiley.com/doi/10.1111/mono.v82.2/issuetoc.

Marc H. Bornstein is Senior Investigator and Head of Child and Family Research at the Eunice Kennedy Shriver National Institute of Child Health and Human Development. His research focuses on child and family development across cultures and brain development.

Noel A. Card is Professor of Human Development and Family Studies at the University of Connecticut. His research focuses on child and adolescent social development as well as developmental methodology.

Pamela Davis-Kean is a Professor of Psychology at the University of Michigan. Her research focuses on the influence of socio-economic status on child development as well as quantitative methodology.

Pega Davoudzadeh is a post-doctoral researcher at the University of California, Davis earning her PhD in quantitative psychology. Her research focuses on modeling longitudinal, multiple-group, categorical data to understand psychological processes.

Britt K. Gorrall is a graduate student in the Research, Evaluation, Measurement, and Statistics concentration within the Educational Psychology

DOI: 10.1111/mono.12304

and Leadership program at Texas Tech University. Her research interests include modern missing data treatments, scale development, latent variable modeling, and organizational culture.

Kevin J. Grimm is Professor of Psychology at Arizona State University. His research focuses on multivariate longitudinal methods for the analysis of change, longitudinal mixture modeling to study divergent development, and early predictor of academic success.

Scott M. Hofer is Professor of Psychology at the University of Victoria. His research focuses on lifespan development and aging as well as developmental research methods.

Justin Jager is an Assistant Professor within the T. Denny Sanford School of Social and Family Dynamics at Arizona State University. His research focuses on individual and family development across the transition to adulthood and developmental methodology.

Todd D. Little is a professor of Educational Psychology and Director of the Institute for Measurement, Methodology, Analysis, and Policy at Texas Tech University. His research encompasses latent variable modeling, modern missing data treatments, action-control processes, aggression, and bullying prevention.

Lawrence Lo is a graduate student in Human Development and Family Studies at Pennsylvania State University. His research focuses time series analysis, Kalman filtering, and structural equation modeling.

Diane L. Putnick is a researcher and statistician with the Child and Family Research Section of the Eunice Kennedy Shriver National Institute of Child Health and Human Development. Her research focuses on child and family development across cultures and developmental methodology.

Nilam Ram is Professor of Human Development & Family Studies and Psychology at Pennsylvania State University. He specializes in longitudinal research methodology and lifespan development—particularly in how capture and modeling of within-person/intraindividual change at multiple time-scales can contribute to our understanding of human behavior.

Michael J. Rovine is Senior Fellow in Human Development and Quantitative Methods at the University of Pennsylvania. His research focuses on developmental methodology, applied statistics, and time series and single subject modeling.

Jonathan Rush is a Doctoral Candidate in the Department of Psychology at the University of Victoria. His research focuses on within-person variations in health and well-being as well as methodology for the analysis of change.

Eugene W. Wang is an Associate Professor in Community, Family, and Addiction Sciences at Texas Tech University. His research focuses on multivariate statistical methods to study disruptive and antisocial behavior in children, adolescents, and adults.

Paul E. Jose received his PhD in Developmental Psychology from Yale University in 1980. He has combined cutting-edge innovations in developmental psychology and research methods in his research and teaching since then. His recent book, *Doing Statistical Mediation and Moderation* (Guilford Press, 2013), was an effort to clarify the procedures for performing two statistical methods that are frequently misunderstood and incorrectly used.

STATEMENT OF EDITORIAL POLICY

The SRCD *Monographs* series aims to publish major reports of developmental research that generates authoritative new findings and that foster a fresh perspective and/or integration of data/research on conceptually significant issues. Submissions may consist of individually or group-authored reports of findings from some single large-scale investigation or from a series of experiments centering on a particular question. Multiauthored sets of independent studies concerning the same underlying question also may be appropriate. A critical requirement in such instances is that the individual authors address common issues and that the contribution arising from the set as a whole be unique, substantial, and well integrated. Manuscripts reporting interdisciplinary or multidisciplinary research on significant developmental questions and those including evidence from diverse cultural, racial, and ethnic groups are of particular interest. Also of special interest are manuscripts that bridge basic and applied developmental science, and that reflect the international perspective of the Society. Because the aim of the *Monographs* series is to enhance cross-fertilization among disciplines or subfields as well as advance knowledge on specialized topics, the links between the specific issues under study and larger questions relating to developmental processes should emerge clearly and be apparent for both general readers and specialists on the topic. In short, irrespective of how it may be framed, work that contributes significant data and/or extends a developmental perspective will be considered.

Potential authors who may be unsure whether the manuscript they are planning wouldmake an appropriate submission to the SRCD *Monographs* are invited to draft an outline or prospectus of what they propose and send it to the incoming editor for review and comment.

Potential authors are not required to be members of the Society for Research in Child Development nor affiliated with the academic discipline of psychology to submit a manuscript for consideration by the *Monographs*. The significance of the work in extending developmental theory and in contributing new empirical information is the crucial consideration.

Submissions should contain a minimum of 80 manuscript pages (including tables and references). The upper boundary of 150–175 pages is more flexible, but authors should try to keep within this limit. Manuscripts must be double-spaced, 12pt Times New Roman font, with 1-inch margins. If color artwork is submitted, and the authors believe color art is necessary to the presentation of their work, the submissions letter should indicate that one or more authors or their institutions are prepared to pay the substantial costs associated with color art reproduction. Please submit manuscripts electronically to the SRCD *Monographs* Online Submissions and Review Site (Scholar One) at http://mc.manuscriptcentral.com/mono. Please contact the *Monographs* office with any questions at monographs@srcd.org.

The corresponding author for any manuscript must, in the submission letter, warrant that all coauthors are in agreement with the content of the manuscript. The corresponding author also is responsible for informing all coauthors, in a timely manner, of manuscript submission, editorial decisions, reviews received, and any revisions recommended. Before publication, the corresponding author must warrant in the submissions letter that the study has been conducted according to the ethical guidelines of the Society for Research in Child Development.

A more detailed description of all editorial policies, evaluation processes, and format requirements can be found under the "Submission Guidelines" link at http://srcd.org/publications/monographs.

Monographs Editorial Office
e-mail: monographs@srcd.org

Editor, Patricia J. Bauer
Department of Psychology, Emory University
36 Eagle Row
Atlanta, GA 30322
e-mail: pjbauer@emory.edu

Note to NIH Grantees

Pursuant to NIH mandate, Society through Wiley-Blackwell will post the accepted version of Contributions authored by NIH grantholders to PubMed Central upon acceptance. This accepted version will be made publicly available 12 months after publication. For further information, see http://www.wiley.com/go/nihmandate.

SUBJECT INDEX

Page numbers in *italics* represent figures.

A
Abelson, Bob, 143–144
accelerated longitudinal design, 131
acceleration as determinant, 58
adaptive test, 78–79
age, 31–33, 69
American Psychological Association (APA), 146, 147
Analysis of Causes (Determinants) of Interindividual Differences in Intra-individual Change, 49–50
Analysis of Causes (Determinants) of Intraindividual Change, 49
Analysis of Interrelationships in Behavioral Change 49, 52
ANOVA, 24–26, 50, 84–86, 117, 128, 142
APA. *See* American Psychological Association
assessment, optimizing, 78–79
attachment research, 33–35
Australasian Human Development Association, 149
autoregressive model, 54, 88–90

B
Baltes and Nesselroade's rationales, 47–50, 123
Bayesian methods, 134–135, 146, 147
beeper study, 41
behavioral factor, 14
between-person differences, 55–57, *56,* 67–70, 72–79, *77*
biological factor, 14
Borkenau and Ostendorf personality data set, 98–100

C
CFA. *See* confirmatory factor analysis
change, 51, 57–58, 67–68, 69–72, 125, 132

CURRENT